T H E
B A L A N C E D   G A R D E N

THE
BALANCED
TOWN, COUNTRY AND COURTYARD

PAUL BANGAY
GARDEN

Photography by
SIMON GRIFFITHS

LANTERN
an imprint of
PENGUIN BOOKS

To Lesley Dunt
for her immense understanding of my designs

Pages 2–3 The two parts of the east room at St Ambrose Farm, looking north.
The garden is featured on pages 136–43.

LANTERN

Published by the Penguin Group
Penguin Group (Australia)
250 Camberwell Road, Camberwell, Victoria 3124, Australia
(a division of Pearson Australia Group Pty Ltd)
Penguin Group (USA) Inc.
375 Hudson Street, New York, New York 10014, USA
Penguin Group (Canada)
90 Eglinton Avenue East, Suite 700, Toronto ON M4P 2Y3, Canada
(a division of Pearson Penguin Canada Inc.)
Penguin Books Ltd
80 Strand, London WC2R 0RL, England
Penguin Ireland
25 St Stephen's Green, Dublin 2, Ireland
(a division of Penguin Books Ltd)
Penguin Books India Pvt Ltd
11 Community Centre, Panchsheel Park, New Delhi – 110 017, India
Penguin Group (NZ)
Cnr Airborne and Rosedale Roads, Albany, Auckland, New Zealand
(a division of Pearson New Zealand Ltd)
Penguin Books (South Africa) (Pty) Ltd
24 Sturdee Avenue, Rosebank, Johannesburg 2196, South Africa

Penguin Books Ltd, Registered Offices: 80 Strand, London WC2R 0RL, England

First published by Penguin Group (Australia), a division of Pearson Australia Group Pty Ltd, 2003
This paperback edition published by Penguin Group (Australia), a division of Pearson Australia Group Pty Ltd, 2005

1 3 5 7 9 10 8 6 4 2

Text copyright © Paul Bangay 2003
Photography copyright © Simon Griffiths 2003

The moral right of the authors has been asserted

Design by Tony Palmer, Penguin Design Studio
Typeset in 9.5 pt Frutiger Condensed by Post Pre-Press, Brisbane
Photography by Simon Griffiths
Scanning and separations by Splitting Image P/L, Clayton, Victoria
Printed and bound in Singapore by Imago Productions

National Library of Australia
Cataloguing-in-Publication data:

Bangay, Paul.
The balanced garden: town, country and courtyard.

Includes index.
ISBN 1 920 98941 2.

1. Gardens – Australia – Design. 2. Landscape gardening –
Australia. I. Griffiths, Simon (Simon John). II. Title.

712.60994

www.penguin.com.au

THE
BALANCED GARDEN

INTRODUCTION

Balance: it's something people feel they
never have enough of today when work and
commitments seem always about to overwhelm
private life. We're always hearing the catchcry
'I need some balance in my life' – but I don't think
people believe a garden designer can deliver
that! Certainly garden owners' briefs to me are
far more modest and, quite understandably, far
more practical: people want to enjoy a number
of activities in their garden and they have fixed
ideas about the materials they would like to use.

Yet although people may not ask themselves
whether a garden can bring them balance,
I know that it can. A garden – a *balanced*
garden – presents people with an aesthetic
of order and regularity. But it also transmits
something more mysterious and emotional:
a sense of harmony, a perception of rightness,
and the deep pleasure of that.

Symmetry and balance are intrinsically related, but there's more at work in the town front garden shown on pages 6–7 than symmetry: restraint of planting and ornamentation too, and an intriguing hint of more garden beyond, make the garden a harmonious experience.

A favourite solution of mine to the problem of incorporating a swimming pool into a small back garden is to make the main ornament a fountain that spills into the pool itself (pages 9 and 10–11). The gardens shown are discussed on pages 38–9 and 102–5.

Questioned more closely about the style of design they like, people who've approached me always say that they prefer a 'classic garden'; by this they mean they like a symmetrical garden. Symmetry – the first characteristic the term 'balanced garden' usually calls to mind – is something people find it easy to relate to. That doesn't surprise me. To my mind a perfectly symmetrical garden is one of the most harmonious gardens possible. Symmetry is rarely found in the natural landscape so to give it form in a garden is an act of imagination. To me garden making is all about the domination of 'civilisation' over 'nature'. (Of course for lots of talented designers introducing symmetry is exactly what gardening is not about.)

Does this idea of garden designing sound too controlling? Perhaps, but it's funny how the individual elements in a formal garden can look manipulated to the point of torture – think of one pot of topiary! – yet when brought together the effect is satisfying.

The most important task for me when designing a garden is to create a major axis. That's my starting point: deciding where to divide the garden to achieve balance. Usually the path to the front door, or a sight-line from the house to a focal point in the back garden, becomes the major axis. Once it's established the rest of the design tends to fall into place.

A central axis, however, doesn't confer perfect symmetry on a garden. Achieving equilibrium can be more a matter of balancing masses on either side of the axis than having the layout of one side mirror the other. In many instances the garden on either side of the major axis cannot be the same: the block may be irregular, the house may sit at an angle or there may be structures such as a garage or a swimming pool to one side. Consequently achieving balance may become a case of introducing a core symmetry that can bind the whole garden. That's what I've done recently at my farm, where the major, east–west axis, running the full length of the property, bisects one part of the garden into what

will become quite different areas – a swimming pool in an expanse of grass on one side and a quite complex formal garden on the other. A walk marks the axis in this part of the garden and I've ensured a core symmetry by setting a privet hedge and a line of tilia trees on either side of it.

In other instances where a symmetrical layout is not possible, the parts to either side of the main axis need to appear to have an equal weight they don't in fact possess. Adding a few small trees on one side can't possibly balance several huge old trees on the other; two new trees can't possibly balance twenty original ones. But balance doesn't necessarily depend on the same number and placement of trees (or ornaments or water features) on both sides of the garden: it very much depends on a visual rather than a literal equipoise. The matching of groups of stone spheres on the floor of the rooftop garden shown at the end of this book to groups of clipped balls of English box in the garden beds above them – that's a matter of weight distribution, not symmetry.

Balance within a garden is not dependent on the size of the area. The symmetrical knot garden shown on page 164 is tiny, but it's perfectly balanced in itself. The hard thing is balancing the size of the garden with the mass of the house. Making a house appear correctly sited – bringing it into equilibrium with the garden – that takes a bit of doing, particularly now that urban houses are getting larger while blocks are getting smaller. It's a matter of proportion: of matching the scale of the garden to the scale of the house. Proportion is always comparative, always about the relationship of one element to another in a design. To exaggerate: you wouldn't have an oversized house with only a row of primulas in front of it. That's not getting the balance right.

Making sure the edges of the building are softened with a low hedge helps. And trees, if there's space for them, can place a house, can make its position seem logical in the garden. Quite often the verticality of a house on a small block is overwhelming so a tree at either end of the façade, or either side of the front door, is a way of bringing down the height of the house and integrating the house with the garden. On page 59 there is a garden in which two pin oaks, as they mature, will balance the substantial house behind them.

And when such a house has a garden that's more the size for primulas? Then the vertical plane of the house itself has to be utilised: a wisteria trained on the wall (or on a pergola), for example, can act in place of a tree. Symmetrically placed cones of lillypilly in pots bridge house and garden in the forecourt shown on page 17, which has little space. Or clever trees can be chosen: trees that don't take up much room; don't have intrusive root systems; and can be espaliered or pleached – treated almost like bonsai, if required – and grown against the boundary (usually a distance of 4 or 5 metres from the house is necessary, although I've grown a row of hornbeams 2 metres from the side of a house quite safely).

Achieving equilibrium can be about balancing contrasting elements, not only mass. Again a sense of proportion is all-important. Take the relationship between lawn and gravel, and gravel and paving in a garden: I would opt for less paving and more lawn because grass is softer to look at; and more gravel than paving for the same reason.

But sometimes balancing the elements in a garden is just not possible, either because the space is intrinsically unbalanced in relation to the building (as a balcony garden is), or because recreational requirements override any other consideration – if there's only room for a desired tennis court, for instance, balance is thrown out straight away. Even so, as a number of the town gardens in this book demonstrate, by screening, by diverting the eye, by employing certain tricks to create an illusion of space, a tennis court – and the lack of balance – may be disguised.

Often people, naturally enough, want to cram too many design elements into too small a space. But a lot going on, literally and aesthetically, makes a design look itsy-bitsy. Restraint and good proportion in all elements of the garden – these are the big things I fight for. Restraint comes from, for example, limiting the number of paths added and the number of features displayed; good proportion comes from making those paths broad and those features substantial – in fact outright overscaling is often crucial to achieving a sense of order and solidity.

In addition to appropriate layout and scale, balance is brought to a garden by the plants that are introduced, their colours and the way they are grouped together; and by the ornaments chosen and their relationship to the garden. When designing a garden, you need to have in mind how you want it to look ultimately. Plants should grow into that vision and nothing past that – which is why the selection of trees is a serious matter. Trees that look good for five years and then fight against the site wreck the whole garden.

A garden is stabilised by restricting planting to strong groupings of a limited number of colours and types. Of all the colours in the garden green for me is the most essential, the most soothing, the most harmonious. Although people often think of it as not so much a colour as a background to colour, it comes in too many different shades and textures and leaf shapes to ever take a secondary place.

I certainly plant roses, hydrangeas and flowering, fruiting deciduous trees, but always within an evergreen framework. And I certainly understand why plantsmen and plantswomen adore every stage of perennials – the whole act of lifting them every third year and dividing them, of putting straw over them in winter and watching them come up in spring, then die down in autumn. There's a side of me too that enjoys the pleasure and challenge of nurturing plants, but it's always in conflict with my designer's desire to have a completed garden from the start.

What I try to give people when they say they want flowers are plants that will provide greenness twelve months of the year, in addition to seasonal flowers – and be hardy as well. In a country where water conservation is such a critical issue, it's essential to grow tough plants that aren't constantly thirsty. That means selecting indigenous plants, and species from other parts of the world – the Mediterranean, for instance – that have conditions similar to those found in Australia. The plants I return to again and again are evergreens such as lillypilly (*Acmena smithii*), English box (*Buxus sempervirens*) and the cycad *Cycas revoluta* that give gardens a look of luxuriance yet can go without water for days. (And deciduous *Wisteria sinensis* doesn't ever seem to need a drink!)

If an evergreen structure brings a sense of permanence to a garden, so too does simplicity of planting, planting en masse. I love those occasions when a site gives me the opportunity to use only two kinds of plant or even one, but lots of that one or two.

I'm at a stage where I'm also paring down ornamentation, to just a plain sphere or obelisk or bench or vase – and when I say vase, it's often just a pot with a citrus tree in it. Very simple, very functional, very striking. And water, for me, has become a sculptural element in the landscape, a material to be manipulated in new ways. I'm trying to avoid decorated mouldings on pools by substituting slabs of stone as ornamentation or taking lawn right up to the edge so that the pool is just a sheet of water. In other cases, as the first garden in 'Town' shows, I'm placing pebbles very close to the surface and running only a thin skin of water over them, with a sole jet of water for ornament. This sets up a play between the texture and colour of the pebbles and the water – and also creates a pool that's safe for children. The Villa Lante in Italy has part of its garden devoted to the usual wonderful statues in the classical style, but another part that appears to be composed only of squares of clipped hedge spurting water: no pools are visible at all. That's perfect ornamentation.

The function of ornaments in the balanced garden is rather different from that of plants. Obviously a pair of urns or fountains offers an effective way of reinforcing symmetry – quite often it may in fact be the only element that lends symmetry to an asymmetrical garden. Primarily, however, a garden ornament acts as the focal point of the major axis and any secondary axes. Consequently it is usually placed at the end of the axis, as the culmination of a journey: its purpose is to lead the eye through the garden, persuading the observer to follow. At my farm I've set an elevated urn at the extreme (boundary) end of the main axis to draw the visitor to its furthest part.

For all the careful equilibrium established, the balanced garden is not a coldly static one. The harmony of the whole depends on movement and emotion. In a large garden, for instance, one room flows into the next: there is always enticement and discovery and tantalising glimpses of garden further on – a lot of emotions are evoked in the well-thought-out garden. Change and variation keep the explorer engaged, that change and variation coming from the different concepts developed in the different rooms, while careful articulation of the main axes ensures that every part of the garden unfolds with an irresistible, if measured, force.

If the balanced garden is logical, it is not totally predictable. There are always serious reasons for any design decision, but the tangible expression of that decision may be unexpected or light-hearted. (In the garden on page 84 the statue in the fountain, which I would normally overscale, is decidedly underscaled, while the fruiting fig trees that form cradles for pots of topiary on page 38 add a whimsical touch to a formal setting.)

At the moment I'm thinking about how to install jets of water – like ones used in sixteenth-century Italian gardens – that will come to life as visitors walk around the farm and step on pressure points. The simplicity of the effect and the relationship that is established between the individual and the garden appeal to me strongly – the playfulness adds another dimension to the balanced garden.

———————

This book, rather like my first, *The Defined Garden*, is an invitation to stroll through a number of recently designed gardens, in this instance to see how balance has been achieved in a variety of situations. The book is divided into 'Town', 'Country' and 'Courtyard', but most of the gardens come under 'Town' because that's where most of us live. All the same many of us now also own places beyond the city, or have made the move from town to country, so I have included several rural and sea-side gardens in 'Country'.

For the purposes of the book I have reserved 'Court-yard' for tiny or difficult areas, even though many of the preceding town and country gardens have a separate part, such as a walled swimming area, that by any general definition of the word would be called a court-yard. The term as it's used in the final part of the book is code for 'unbalanced': for light wells and other snippets of garden – including two rooftops – that have intrinsic problems of space, position, soil, light or ventilation.

If the gardens in 'Courtyard' self-evidently have limitations so too can even the least likely ones, the biggest gardens. Garden builders are never free to develop their perfect plan without reference to the house architecture, the setting, the needs of plants and the intended uses of the space. Balance is always a negotiated outcome in gardens – but always worth striving for because of the aesthetic and emotional harmony it brings to people's lives.

TOWN

The reality of designing town gardens these days is that outdoor lifestyles and technological advances are putting increasing pressure on the garden at the very time that blocks are becoming smaller. People want everything! Everyone wants to dine outdoors, and often they want to swim and play tennis also. They usually want parking for several cars or even an automated underground garage. And if they have children, the children must have space for riding bikes, roller-blading and ball games as well as for the traditional sandpit, swing and climbing frame.

The challenge for the designer of town gardens, then, is to take into account a number of diverse factors and make a number of disparate elements work together in a limited space – and when technology is one of these factors, and recreation another, and the aesthetics of a stress-free environment a third, it can be quite exciting.

The designer of town gardens starts with practicalities: how to accommodate cars, how to move people into and through the garden, how to incorporate recreational areas — not to mention how to include heating units, bins, washing lines, barbecues . . . Translated into terms of achieving a balanced design, this means ensuring the house is well sited on its block; softening the dominance of house and hard surfaces; and disguising the space limitations of the block and the pressures on it.

Ensuring that the house is sited well means firstly making the driveway and paths — the main flow of traffic — logical. A drive takes up a lot of space, given its ideal width is 3–3.5 metres; a garage even more. Hiding the cars or making the garden look as though it's not all drive becomes one of the most pressing challenges.

When space in a front garden is limited, people are often in competition with cars. It is usually assumed both need separate entries, but this doesn't have to be the case (for instance, there is no reason why a security gate for cars can't be operated by intercom and double as an entry for people). Of course a single entry only succeeds if visitors don't come straight up against a car, but step instead into an attractive forecourt.

The most direct route is not always the best route! Quite often diverting people makes a garden look larger and more interesting, and the arrival at the front door more of an event. The axis from a central front gate to a central front door has such fundamental strength that I would always want to develop the design along it. Even so, a low intersecting feature such as a central pool or a garden bed that people have to walk around can nicely prolong an otherwise short, uneventful journey.

It's sometimes not apparent from the architecture of the house where the house entrance is, so it's the job of the garden design to make sure people are delivered in a well-mannered way to the front door. There can be secondary paths but it needs to be obvious that they are not going to the front door — they need to clearly end at a garden seat or an urn, for example. The logic of the garden must always be apparent, even if the front door is not.

It's a common mistake to make the main path (and the secondary ones) too narrow. In a small front garden an overscaled path paradoxically makes the garden look larger. Clever adjustments to the ground plan need to be made to compensate for the space lost, but a wide main path gives the garden — and the house — more presence than the standard 1-metre-wide path ever could.

Terraces are essential to siting a house properly within its garden. They are the feet of the building; visually they balance the house. And psychologically a transition is needed between the sheltered world of the house and the more exposed environment of the garden. I think the minimum depth for a dining terrace should be 4 metres — enough for people to push their chairs back from a table without falling off the edge. And anything less looks out of proportion to the bulk of a house.

A pergola links house and garden further; it allows an architectural element of the house — perhaps a building material, a decorative detail or the colour of a trim — to be taken into the garden. Crucially a pergola helps to bring down the height of the house visually. Quite often a two-storey house looms over its small garden; a pergola, like trees symmetrically planted in front of the façade, breaks up the verticality.

These days children — and their parents — frequently have much more need of a hard surface than a traditional lawn. Often in a town garden the outdoor eating area has to double as the play space, and adjacent plants have to be tough ones grown a couple of metres back from the action. It's quite a difficult feat keeping an unbroken expanse of hard surface in proportion to the other elements of the garden. Not that it's an intrinsic problem: if the paving design is good the horizontal surface looks interesting in itself, and it can be broken up further with tubs and outdoor furniture. However, there must be enough planted garden to compensate for the hard surface. Usually a complex arrangement of flowerbeds is out of the question, and beds must be pushed to the boundaries. If they're made too narrow, that's when everything goes wrong. They need to be at least 1.5 metres wide to allow for a layered planting that will make them look deeper than they are and not as if they've been squeezed against the boundaries. The eye needs to be taken on a measured journey from low plants to medium plants to tall ones that hide the fence.

A tennis court adds another bare, hard surface. The average size is 31–33 metres by 15.5–17.5 metres and it must be aligned north–south: big demands of a garden. It has to be enclosed on all sides by a fence to a minimum height of 3 metres, and even its tall lights are ugly and intrusive. However, the artificial grass surfaces of today's tennis courts can be used for other sports, not excluding roller-blading; and a court can usually be built to the back boundary line. The far end of the garden is definitely the best place for a large amenity not used much of the time. The main trick, though, is to disguise the court. Using sideline draw nets that can be pulled back like curtains helps, as does a barrier planting to a height of about 1.5 metres that suggests the court is a continuation of the garden.

Swimming pools are less likely to unbalance the design because they are not as big and water is more interesting than a court surface. Nevertheless increasingly there are electronically controlled features and equipment, such as swim jets, that interfere with the clean lines of a pool. Automated pool covers are not just for heat conservation: people are rightly anxious about children drowning and want to keep the cover on except when the pool is in use – so the beauty of the water is lost most of the time. In contrast, the compulsory safety fence (to a height of at least 1.2 metres) is easy to make attractive since the building material can be attractive: a match with the house and garden walls; invisible glass; or a fine metal against which a hedge can be planted to suggest a garden room. To help integrate swimming pool and garden, it's worth considering having a smaller or narrower pool than the standard 12-metre by 5-metre one – perhaps a lap pool – and foregoing that always under-used amenity, the spa. And if a spa must be added, let it look like an ornamental pool instead.

Most urban blocks, unlike country gardens, do not have the space to be divided into separate rooms that open into each other; their back and front gardens can really only read as single spaces. This is where simplicity comes into play: a simplicity of layout, materials, colour and ornamentation that ensures scale and proportion are right.

Visually stretching the space is also crucial to achieving a sense of balance in town gardens. A change of level – even if the 'terrace' created is little more than a raised planter box – adds interest to the layout and the illusion of space where there is little. And, as already mentioned, a stepped boundary planting can effectively make the perimeter disappear, suggesting that the garden is larger than it is. The tiers can become a lush background to a feature placed at the far end of the garden or to something happening on the dining terrace – to a handsome table and chairs perhaps that deflect attention from the boundaries.

Creating focal points at eye level within the garden psychologically blocks out neighbouring buildings, while blurring the boundaries physically reinforces this. Australian streetscapes can be a discordant mixture of house styles, a mock-Tudor house sitting next to a south-of-France villa or a tall apartment block, so that often it is very necessary for the garden to turn in on itself.

Other elements – water, lighting – complete the sense of a private, harmonious world, more expansive than it is in reality and separated from the most jarring aspects of city life. The sound of moving water disguises the noise of traffic, and often at night soft garden lights counteract the distracting lights of passing cars. Balance is possible.

EVEN IN THOSE exceptional instances
where a town garden, like this one, has considerable
space, the design can't be an entity in itself. It's a fundamental of balance that the garden be in harmony with
the house it surrounds.

Nothing but the boldest, most minimal, most symmetrical front garden design could match the weight,
restraint and symmetry of this house, with its massive
stone portico and high rendered walls pierced only by
rectangles of glass. Accordingly I set two very plain, very
large, 3-metre by 3-metre raised pools in two larger
squares of lawn on either side of a central path – firmly
in proportion to the house and the size of the space.

A strong, single jet of water was all the movement
the two pools required in a setting where traditional
ornamentation would have been out of place. Big brown
pebbles – brown to add richness to the pale render of
the pools and the house – seem virtually to float on top
of the pools, covered only by the merest film of water.

The fact that the front area is extensive was irrelevant to the planting: like the garden layout, the planting
had to be true to the strength and simplicity of the house.
Bands of lightly trimmed creeping juniper (*Juniperus
horizontalis*) around perimeters and pools tie the garden
together – the juniper chosen to meet the owners'
preference for loose, informal hedging and, like the grass,
to soften the architecture a little.

At the back of the house is a courtyard that is
highly visible through glass doors the moment you enter
the front hall. Because it's not used a great deal (most
outdoor living takes place in a long side garden), its
need for a dramatic design could be met with a huge
(8-metre by 8-metre) ornamental pool taken almost to
the house and boundary walls (see pages 24–5).

AGAINST THE HOUSE

*a creeping juniper hedge encloses gardenias. Beneath
the pear trees (Pyrus calleryana 'Bradford') that screen
the neighbours on one side and the house's main, side
garden on the other, the juniper and gardenias are
augmented by azaleas in a white and green garden
of some unity.*

The owners love the lily ponds of Bali so in the courtyard we created a lily pond on which were moored six stepping stones in the form of 600-millimetre by 1.2-metre pavers. Between each paver, on either side, a jet of water leaps 600 millimetres into the air. As in the front garden, moving water at its most elemental is all the ornamentation that this style of house can take and remain balanced. It allows the courtyard to be appropriately austere, without in any way being harsh.

A series of recreational spaces, including a sunken tennis court and a swimming pool, were already in place, making the side, main garden intrinsically asymmetrical to work with. The size of this garden, however, did make it possible to plant a number of trees in scale with both the house and the only original tree on the property, a fine 100-year-old elm. A hedge of Hill's weeping fig trees (*Ficus microcarpa* var. *hillii*) was planted along the street boundary; *Magnolia grandiflora* 'Little Gem' went into constructed planter boxes to mark the corners of the pool terrace; and the deep flowerbeds beyond the elm gained several *Magnolia grandiflora*. The architect had sited the pool to be overlooked from the dining-room windows. Extending the sight-line that ran from the windows, down a flight of stairs and then the length of the pool, I placed in the bed beyond a very big *Phoenix canariensis* palm — the ultimate feature in a garden where ornamentation could be decidedly large and striking but never elaborate.

A CLIPPED HEDGE OF
Prunus lusitanica, *with* Trachelospermum asiaticum *beneath, separates the swimming-pool terrace from the sunken tennis court in the side, main garden. To allow people relaxing around the pool to feel part of the garden, glass was used for the safety fence.*

Jets of water can be stunningly lit at night (previous pages). The uplighting of the four Japanese maples that mark the corners of a quiet part to one side of the ornamental pool in the back courtyard is fittingly softer.

THE SIDEWAY that commonly carries people (and possibly wheelbarrows and bikes) from the front to the back of an ordinary-sized town property presents the garden designer with problems. It's often an intrinsically unbalanced area – narrow and overshadowed by high house and boundary walls – yet as the only external thoroughfare it needs both to provide comfortable access and to 'look presentable'.

The sideway of the garden that follows is only about 3 metres wide and perhaps 20 metres long but, in addition to being the only external link between back and front, it is overlooked by a number of important rooms, including the dining room, so its function is not merely utilitarian. And to compound the difficulties, all soil had been removed when an underground garage was constructed, most of which could not be replaced because the weight would have been too great. Paving the whole sideway appeared the only option.

The design task, as I saw it, was to break up the extreme length and straight lines without impeding traffic; to transcend the problems of width by exploiting the vertical plane; and to work with a limited number of hard and soft materials but push their uses to the maximum.

To soften the unremitting hard surfaces and provide visual interest for the rooms facing the sideway, we built planter boxes along the boundary wall, leaving bays between them. In two of these bays we set large tubs of English box (*Buxus sempervirens*) – these protruded sufficiently to add some curve to the straight lines of the sideway without interfering with the passage of people. A third, central bay, which had the most substance – due to its treatment rather than to its actual space – faced the dining-room windows and became the setting for a water feature consisting of a bronze fountain mounted on a backing wall, with a narrow, semicircular trough beneath. Its finely wrought,

entwined dolphins (reproduced from an antique fountain) and its niche within what appears to be a high wall of greenery give the water feature considerable presence, yet it required little width.

The paving in this alleyway was bound to dominate, yet I deliberately extended it to other surfaces. Pavers became the facing and capping for the planter boxes and fountain trough, and edged the fountain-back, refining the surfaces of these structures while unifying the small space and simplifying the materials introduced. This worked because their blandness was counteracted by the introduction of brown and white pebbles: on the horizontal surface as a circle in front of the fountain and on the vertical plane as a crisscross pattern decorating the fountain-back.

The planter boxes could take no width or variety of plant material, but two tiers of hedging disguise this. Severely clipped box became the lower tier, severely clipped lillypilly (*Acmena smithii*) the higher. The two occupy virtually the same vertical plane, yet the effect of the dense, evergreen foliage and the two greens is one of depth and richness. Only the hardiest of plants can cope with such taxing treatment, but the box and lillypilly are thriving. Boston ivy (*Parthenocissus tricuspidata*) on the boundary wall completed the planting. Like the bronze dolphins, a wisp of creeper sneaking under the lip of the fountain added a little pagan playfulness in a tightly controlled area.

The design solutions for the sideway became the design solutions for the adjacent back courtyard, even though the space available (roughly 8 metres by 8 metres) and its intended use were quite different. The courtyard (see pages 30–1) was required primarily to be a paved and uncluttered play area for children. Consequently the main feature – an urn – was pushed right to the back wall and all planting restricted to the

IN A FUNDAMENTALLY *unbalanced garden space the boundary wall, with its fountain and two tiers of planting, provides a counterpoise to the high side wall of the house (opposite page).*

margins. A lovely sense of space resulted. But an unbroken surface of pale pavers would have been boring so inlaid diamonds of the same pebbles used in the sideway alternate with diagonally placed square pavers. Straight perimeter beds would also have been uninteresting so I gave them a quoin design – an outline like that of the cornerstones down a building – in a variation of the recessing in the sideway, but this time delineated just by box hedging, not planters.

The main event in the garden is created by the satyr-adorned urn, standing nearly 3 metres high, which the owner and I chose together. Tucked as it is, like the side fountain, into a wall of greenery, the huge urn makes the garden look long established. The scale of the piece is in keeping with the two-storey house, but at the same time I worked against that by slightly obscuring the urn with foliage. Fine classical urns were traditionally treated in this manner in French landscape architecture so it's a play on an old idea: a useful old idea because the urn – or perhaps I should say the satyr – doesn't leap out at the viewer too much in the small area. The naturalness of the setting prevents the urn from seeming too artificial for a town courtyard, and the face of the satyr peering through the fringe of foliage enhances the subtly pagan atmosphere that began in the sideway.

Again planting was tiered to enrich the setting without competing with the central feature. Here three layers were possible. Behind the box edging pleached Hill's weeping fig trees rise above 'Alba Magnifica' azaleas, which add delicate white flowers in spring to the permanent greens of the garden. The weeping fig is clipped fairly hard, like the box, but allowed to soften a little around the urn.

IN DAYTIME THE SATYR
on the urn in the back courtyard, like the satyrs of classical myth, rests in a 'forest' of green, only half-observed by visitors who stray into the garden; but at night, uplit, he seems to emerge from his forest to preside over the revels (previous pages).

The main event in the garden is created by the satyr-adorned urn, standing nearly 3 metres high, which the owner and I chose together.

BALANCE IS NOT always assured even when a garden is designed and constructed at the same time as its house and in close consultation with the architect. The house shown on the following pages is on quite a large block, but the design challenges were daunting: a magnificent view of Sydney Harbour had to be retained at all cost; the garden area was essentially one long, steep ascent from street to front door; a venerable tree, perhaps 80 years old, had to be preserved; and an underground tunnel built for cars meant only parts of the ascent retained their soil or could take the weight of a lot of imported soil. Not a design and construction job to rush into without careful consideration of all the options and their engineering aspects. Quite a few proposals were tossed backwards and forwards to get the levels right and find the best way to make the house work visually.

The ascent was divided into four levels, the top one a narrow terrace leading to the front door, with flights of stairs between each – about thirty steps in all. It is quite a long haul up the slope for visitors on foot and they could easily have felt overwhelmed by a single flight of stairs; I thought they needed moments in which to pause and look around and be delighted with what they found. With the design that evolved, people always have before them the prospect of a lovely terrace (see page 35). The levels on the ascent could only consist of paving – different configurations of pavers and loose gravel were eventually chosen – with some peripheral planting. However, on either side of the second set of stairs Chinese elms (*Ulmus parvifolia*) were able to be planted, which will eventually arch over to create the illusion of an entry to a new, different room.

Because there needed to be so many steps, we widened the first two flights and fanned them out. In this way they became less confining than narrow flights. The result was stairs that provide an appropriately grand introduction to the house, but also lessen the harsh impact of the retaining walls.

Standing at the gate, waiting to be admitted, visitors hear the faint sound of water falling somewhere. As they climb the sound becomes stronger and they catch sight of a fountain further up. But when they reach the fountain they find that, impressive though it is, this terrace is not the culmination of their journey for off to one side, not visible from below, is a flight of steps to the house terrace. It is only when they have ascended these that the full magnificence of the house's harbour view is revealed.

The fountain is set against a wall capped with the sandstone pavers used throughout, which arches to form its back (see pages 34–5). The water feature itself is about 2.5 metres long, although only about 1.2 metres wide. It consists simply of half a large cement bowl set against a backing of more sandstone pavers, above a trough capped with the same. The proportions and weight of the fountain are in keeping with the house, but the simplicity acknowledges that the main show is the convent spire, with wide water and the city skyline and Sydney Harbour Bridge beyond.

Lines of *Murraya paniculata* define retaining walls and a band follows the outline of the fountain wall. On either side of the fountain, contained in constructed planter boxes, are Indica azaleas. Low hedges of murraya mark either side of a 5-metre-wide lawn extending between the fountain courtyard and the edge of the property. At the boundary a hedge of Hill's weeping fig trees, kept tightly under control, blocks out an ugly nearby roof while leaving the harbour view from the lawn unimpeded.

Because of its glorious view, the house was pushed as far back on the block as possible to maximise space in the front garden. Since the block has been carved out of

AS THE VISITOR ASCENDS,

a substantial fountain on a terrace higher up comes
into view from the first of the four terraces leading
to the house in this garden (above).

When the fountain terrace has been left behind
and the last terrace, in front of the house, is finally
reached, all of Sydney Harbour seems to lie beyond.

the slope, which continues to climb behind it, the back of the house looks straight onto a massive retaining wall, only 3 or 4 metres away. I decided to divide this boundary wall into two, necessarily narrow, stepped terraces. The lower of the two, about 900 millimetres above the courtyard and only about 600 millimetres wide, now contains a hedge of murraya with a line of the climber *Trachelospermum asiaticum*, which I like to use as a ground cover, at its feet, and climbing fig (*Ficus pumila*) behind it. The higher level, 1 metre wide, also holds a murraya hedge, but with a row of Hill's weeping fig trees planted behind and Boston ivy climbing against the wall. The tall fig trees were planted because a neighbouring house looms beyond and the only way to give the narrow garden privacy was to plant a hedge, since regulations prevented any vertical extension of the retaining wall. Quite a lot of planting altogether in a very restricted spot – but careful selection of plants has ensured six lush tiers of greenery.

At ground level, opposite the French doors of the dining room, I set a second fountain. The bowl chosen was the same as the one at the front of the house, but this time left as a full circle and placed on a low rendered-brick base. Where water softly overflows from bowl to trough in the first fountain, here it gently gushes from a central jet.

Achieving balance in the courtyard didn't come easily, but the wall of different greens and different textures has turned a potentially oppressive area into an appropriately intimate backdrop to dining.

ON A SUMMER'S DAY,
with the dining-room doors to the rear courtyard wide open, people at the table eat and talk to the sound of water spilling in the background (opposite page).

Achieving balance in the courtyard didn't come easily, but the wall of different greens and different textures has turned a potentially oppressive area into an appropriately intimate backdrop to dining.

*fruiting figs holds a dome of box in
a huge pot on either side of the central
path: a whimsical touch in a seriously
symmetrical front garden
(opposite page).*

NOT HAVING A FENCE is an excellent way of making a shallow front garden look spacious. This small neo-Georgian house doesn't have a front fence so I could design a very broad path to the front portico, wider than a single gate and wider than the steps to the house. Such a path would have been over-powering in a totally enclosed garden. Without a barrier between it and the streetscape, the path has the visual effect of stretching the front garden markedly.

As a consequence I could herald the approach to the house with three squares of clipped English box planted in the path on both sides – quite a gesture, but in no way pretentious. The broadness of the path would have left it still looking slightly under-designed so I added a herringbone-patterned band of bricks down the centre of the pale pavers. The bricks of the pattern are lighter coloured than those of the house, which would have been a little oppressive.

Symmetry was established with the treatment of the path, and I was able to extend that symmetry to the rest of the front garden. The area in fact is not square, but one side contains a car ramp that needed to be screened off, and when this was achieved with a hedge of Hill's weeping fig trees (matched on the other side with a second one), a space of 10 metres by 10 metres was left. The main surface of this area became gravel, with a square bed set symmetrically either side of the path.

The two beds were defined with box, trimmed to a height of 300 millimetres. Within each square I planted a higher square of fruiting fig trees (*Ficus carica*), which act as a cradle for an elevated, 1-metre-high cement pot containing a dome of box, to be kept to a height of about 800 millimetres. I like the lively shape and the size of the fig leaves, which contrast so well with the tight box: they look like hands holding up the pots of topiary. The figs have to be clipped hard – large, sprawling fig

trees were definitely not part of the plan – but even so they do bear fruit. I find the whole conceit pleasing and rather amusing.

The final task was to prevent a harsh juxtaposition of house and gravel surface. I decided on a 'proper' hedge, to window height, not just a ribbon of green. This allowed glossy-leaved Hill's weeping fig to be used again, and ensured the hedge reached the required height quickly in comparison with slow-growing box.

The back garden of this house is shown at the beginning of the book, on page 9. Essentially it is a courtyard with a swimming pool. The pool is visible from the front door so it was important to incorporate it in an attractive design that also acknowledged the lengthy central axis. Consequently I designed a plinth, to be built into the pool on its long, far side, on which to display a special urn. However, it was not the urn but the plinth itself that was intended to form the fountain. The plinth was plumbed, and a bronze spout set just above the waterline so that the splash would be gentle, not annoying. (And if the owners want or need to move the precious urn in the future, they can do so.) The broad plinth was designed to sit only about 200 millimetres above the pool, but the urn is elevated considerably above that because it came with its own narrower, carved pedestal.

The picture formed by fountain and pool was completed with a backdrop of pleached Hill's weeping fig, grown quite tall to block out some ugly rooftops, and murraya planted below. The two types of plant are a successful combination: weeping fig is quite competitive for water and soil, but murraya can withstand this. (A root-control barrier must be installed in any poolside bed that is to take Hill's weeping fig.) The murraya is trimmed but still manages to produce flowers that perfume the air, making the pool and courtyard a delightful place to be in summer.

AN ELABORATE formal garden, in response to an owner's request: the design that evolved made full use of the opportunity and of a large back area. For the garden's centrepiece I designed a raised ornamental pool as a square with cut-out corners, outlined in English box, in the middle of a larger square of lawn. Each corner of the lawn received squares of clipped box. Half-spheres of box became 'finials' at the centre of these, and at the corners of the pool also. Against a background of weeping lillypilly (*Waterhousia floribunda*), two parterre beds were created on either side of the centrepiece, separated from it by paving. A dark green, glazed French vase was added to the middle of each parterre bed to hold a large ball of box, in a repetition of the centrepiece's box domes: apart from being chosen for their decorative quality, the vases of box were introduced as a bridge between the heights of fountain and side hedges, and to echo the verticality of adjacent balustrade piers.

The back of the house after renovation became one large living area for which I designed a broad dining terrace and a magnificently wide central staircase leading down to the garden (see pages 42–3). On either side of the stairs I ranked, in descending order, clipped weeping lillypilly, gardenias, *Trachelospermum asiaticum*, more gardenias, and box. The steps were continued beyond sphere-topped balustrade piers to ultimately be flanked by constructed square planter boxes containing a frame of clipped box 'supporting' Anduze pots of white geraniums. The glazed pots, being closer to the stairs and the banked planting, were raised higher than their counterparts in the side parterre beds — a necessary balancing of masses in a garden of many elements.

A WIDE BOWL WITH

a single jet of water is the central feature of the back garden. The design of this section of the garden is quite complex, yet the components, with their strong emphasis on plant material and repeated curves and squares, are simple and in keeping with the contemporary lines of the renovated house.

THE 12-METRE-WIDE STAIRS

that descend from a deep terrace to the back
garden were softened with bands of Lonicera nitida.
The dazzling, almost abstract effect created by white
steps and green risers would have been dissipated
if heavy ornamentation had been added to the
balustrade piers: two granite spheres, repeating the
shape of the topiary in the garden, were enough.

The unrenovated back garden contained a kidney-
shaped swimming pool and a tennis court. The
swimming pool was given the straight lines of the
new ornamental pool and parterre beds, and long,
paver-clad steps in keeping with the stairway;
a hedge of weeping lillypilly, matching the ones
planted on the sides of the garden, soon hid
the court (previous pages).

SOMETIMES BRINGING a design into harmony with its setting means linking it to an existing part of the garden – in this instance a wonderful old Edna Walling design, classified by the National Trust. Sadly not a great number of the gardens built by Edna Walling, one of Australia's foremost twentieth-century designers, exist in their entirety so it was a very special project for me to plan a back section in sympathy with the largely intact other parts of her design: a front garden with formal rose beds and a sundial, and a side garden with a reflective ornamental pool.

The back garden had almost fallen into disuse by the time I saw it, and all that remained of Edna Walling's work was a low retaining wall: this I was careful to keep, but the rest of the back needed a completely new life. A recently added garage had created a wing to one side of the house, leaving a square of perhaps 20 metres by 20 metres – the best of starts for a garden.

I wanted to link the back to the larger garden quite fundamentally by continuing the lawn found in the other parts. And since there were no children needing to run around on it, there was no reason to push all the main features to the perimeters, although we did build a generous terrace, onto which the sitting room opens, and a long, 3-metre-deep flowerbed against the back fence.

For the centre of the lawn I designed a raised ornamental pool that was essentially a square with the corners nipped out and a moulded coping to soften its lines. While it was not a repetition of the Edna Walling pool in the side garden – that one is long and rectangular and doesn't have a raised lip – it does convey a sense that the same components have been used. In particular the fountain constructed in the middle reflected the influence of her pool. It took the form of a refined, elongated figure in acknowledgement of the figure on top of a tall column in the Edna Walling design.

In the flowerbed we planted a pleached hedge of Manchurian pear trees (*Pyrus ussuriensis*) to block out the neighbours, with beneath them a collection of perennials and annuals – foxgloves, roses and other flowering plants dear to Edna Walling – to tie the back garden to the other parts. Edna Walling of course frequently introduced flowering, fruiting deciduous trees into her designs, and certainly used Manchurian pears on occasion, although they have perhaps become more common in Australia in recent years.

What puts my own minor stamp on this garden, I guess, are the proportions of the back area, with its somewhat overscaled pond; the use of highly clipped and controlled plants such as the double English box hedges lining the flowerbed, the pleached pear trees and the cones of box marking the corners of the pool; and the formal layout – although any study of Edna Walling's superb ground plans will show how classicist many of her own layouts were. Her designs were much inspired by those of the Italian Renaissance gardens she had studied in books, but because her planting schemes were so soft and spilling it's not always recognised just how architectural her plans were.

It was a privilege to be linked to the tradition of Australian garden making and to someone so important within that tradition – and to work in a garden that had survived many of the ravages of time.

THE SQUARE BACK-GARDEN *space allowed a satisfyingly symmetrical layout (opposite page). The pool and fountain are more elaborate than some I have designed recently, but the use of living material (cones of box) for ornamentation lightens the formality – and links the pool to the garden.*

WORKING WITH the owners and the architect to fit both a house extension and a garden at the back of this house was very much a juggling act, a matter of balancing inside and outside requirements, but a much more rewarding process than dealing with the usual 'Whatever's left over from the house you can have for the garden'.

The owners intended to use the extension as a sitting room, in which they wanted to be constantly aware of the garden. For the garden itself they specified only two things: it must be able to seat a number of people at a table – which effectively meant it must have a large terrace adjacent to the house – and it must have ornamental water. The Victorian character of the house had dictated a conservative garden at the front to match its façade, but made no such demand of the back. Quite the contrary: it was the architecture of the extension that the design needed to be sensitive to. It called for a contemporary garden, with strong lines and restrained ornamentation (water would be perfect). The garden would be viewed principally from three points: from the very front of the house, via the long main hallway and the new sitting room; from a standing or seated position within the sitting room; and from the new dining terrace. Three points on essentially the same sight-line.

An important part of the design process became deciding what kind of windows to have and where to place them. We realised that garden and sitting room would flow together best if the extension was designed as a wide wing, with the back garden wrapping around it on one side and windows looking into both back and side. French doors would open to the side, but the rear wall of the sitting room would be filled instead by a 'picture window'– an expanse of glass set in timber that literally frames the rear garden.

The slope of the land allowed a change of level to be introduced – always one of the most effective ways to make a garden interesting. As I've said, a level change can be made even when the space available is not great, as was the case with this back garden, which measures about 10 metres by 8.5 metres. The terrace created was essentially just a large platform to display an ornamental pool and fountain and built at the far end of the garden in acknowledgement of the main sight-line. The elevation of the feature ensured that it would be visible even to people seated inside the house; set at floor level it would have been obscured by foreground objects.

A deep, central recess in the platform permitted two short flights of parallel steps to ascend on either side. I think it's important that people feel they can explore any part of a garden, but in reality the platform was little more than a support for the 3-metre by 3-metre pool, balanced by two balls of English box on either side. Quite a large area of water for such a small garden, yet the overscaling works because the upper terrace has been made the focus of the whole garden. A substantial, unadorned bowl placed at the centre of the pool appears to be floating on the water: the bowl's base, like the pool's interior, was painted black so that it is not possible to see the support. Just a single column of water spouts in the bowl, and an equally simple curtain of water drops down the centre of the recessed wall into a slot in the paving below.

The fall of water from upper to lower terrace was intended to integrate the two. Planting carried this further. Lines of the pear tree *Pyrus calleryana* 'Bradford' were planted in box-bordered beds along the perimeters, at both levels, to screen the garden from the neighbouring apartment blocks. These pear trees are deciduous but lose their leaves only briefly. Here they were pleached, against a background of Boston ivy, to allow *Hydrangea macrophylla* 'Blue Wave' to be grown

PEOPLE CAN CHANGE
their perspective of the back garden if they wish by climbing the stairs on either side, but they tend not to because the upper terrace is so clearly the stage for a play of water (opposite page).

underneath. It's a luxuriant combination, pear trees, hydrangeas, Boston ivy and box, but it's also a highly practical one. The pears don't create difficult dark, dry areas but do provide just enough shade to protect the hydrangeas, and the box helps to soften the effect of the hydrangeas when they are out of leaf and cut back.

The pavers used were pale, 1-metre by 1-metre cement ones. Instead of laying them on the diagonal with a border around the whole, in Victorian fashion, I set them in a grid, softened slightly by small cut-out squares filled with pebbles. Although the sitting room and dining terrace were planned in conjunction with each other, the pavers used inside and outside were not the same: the owners wanted a warm donkey brown for the sitting room, which was too dark to extend outside, so we chose pavers in a lighter but compatible colour and donkey-brown pebbles for the inserts.

Lighting was crucial for this garden because of the expanse of glass looking into it. All the trunks of the pear trees were uplit, creating fantastical shapes at the edges of the garden. And the upper terrace became truly a stage at night. The steps leading up to it were lit, for both aesthetic and safety reasons; the pond was lit; the underside of the huge bowl was lit. And within the bowl a globe was placed to catch the leaping water, for light on moving water is one of the most dramatic effects in the night garden. In contrast the lower terrace needed only ambient light to softly illuminate a dinner party.

The last task was to design the side part of the back garden. What to frame in the sitting-room French doors? A competing fountain wasn't an option. Nor were statues or urns: too obvious, too weighty for the space, too over-stated for this garden.

The solution was to inset three panels in the high, rendered boundary wall, making the view from all three French doors very directed. Into the panels I had a geo-metric pattern chiselled sufficiently deep to be thickly filled by the small, evergreen leaves of tenacious climbing fig (see pages 52–3). The pattern of the panels is an echo of espalier work I had added in the front garden, but the stiffly upturned 'branches' make it far more iconic.

Symmetry and formalism have very much been put to the use of a contemporary design in this garden. It's contemporary not in the sense that it's starkly minimalist – it isn't. The plan is quite multi-layered and contains a number of elements. Besides it's a domestic design, and most people want their home to be not quite as cutting-edge as a public development. But it is contemporary in the sense that it relies on strong planes, strips ornamen-tation to the bare minimum – just a bowl on a sheet of water and creeper-filled incisions on a side wall – and limits the variety of plants employed.

THE ELEGANT TABLE

and chairs on the lower terrace are to one side
so as not to impede the view of the main feature.
We started the paving on the far side of the terrace
and worked towards the house so that if a row
of pavers had to be cut it would end up adjacent
to the rear wall: a house should always look as
though it has been fitted into the landscape.

THE PATTERN DEVISED

for the side wall panels visible through the sitting-room's French doors: the climbing fig that fills the geometric design is planted in a raised bed of clipped Trachelospermum asiaticum (above). At night concealed downlights wash the whole wall with light, turning the climbing fig to deep shadow. (All parts of the pattern would not have been visible if the panels had been uplit.)

Like the vertical plane, the horizontal surface needed definition, achieved by extending the paving pattern of the main part of the back garden to the side.

THE REGULARITY of the Parisian-style façade seen on the preceding pages demanded a symmetrical garden design, although the form that symmetry took was dependent on the distinctive siting of the house on its block and on the owners' taste. The owners, who are European, didn't want a conventional, highly planted front garden; and they had placed their house about two-thirds back on what is a good-sized, but not exceptionally big, inner-urban block to ensure a long front view of the house from the street.

So perspective was all, and the reason why we planted two lines of that tree most evocative of Europe, the lime or linden, on either side of a straight path to the front door, composed of large (800-millimetre by 800-millimetre) pavers. (The species chosen was the rather upright *Tilia cordata*, not the common *T. x europaea*.) There's a decided air of an avenue – part-illusion of course on a town block where only five pairs of trees were possible.

The tilias were stood in spritely squares of clipped English box. Apart from that the only planting was two boundary lines of pleached hornbeams (*Carpinus betulus*) for privacy. The rest of the front garden became pale gravel right to the front door – quite a bold move, but the pavers of the front path are strongly directional and friendly underfoot and there's no reason for visitors to stray beyond (or carry gravel into the house). The gravel is extraordinarily practical and low-maintenance, just as the owners wanted: it's kept immaculate with a leaf-blower, and it suppresses weeds, keeps moisture in and was comparatively cheap and easy to lay.

The total uniformity of the front garden's horizontal surface was in fact dependent on the kind of gravel employed, for part of the left-hand side is occupied by the lid of an underground garage: to disguise the lid, we needed a gravel that would adhere to it – and only the finest of gravels does that.

What was left of the property for the back garden was more like a courtyard space. However, as well as a terrace for entertaining on, the owners wanted a swimming pool. Inevitably it would have dominated the courtyard so the ruse was to make it a grand pool, worthy of all the attention. The ground slopes up from the house, which allowed the green-tiled pool to be sited on a raised terrace, and I could run two steps nearly the full length of the pool. These steps I lined with green bands of *Lonicera nitida* – the effect is quite mesmerising in the intense light of a summer's day.

Behind the pool, centrally placed so that it could be seen not only from the back sitting room but also as soon as people step inside the front door, I placed a fountain-back – massive but in proportion to house and pool. Its outsized fountain bowl was made on site; into it water spills from a lion's head. The simplicity of bowl and lion's head enhances the monumentality of the fountain while at the same time ensuring that the fountain harmonises rather than competes with two reproduction sphinxes introduced to flank the steps leading up to the pool. The owners favoured sphinxes for the ornamentation, and sphinxes seemed appropriate for the sophisticated courtyard they envisaged. On either side of the fountain, to mitigate the hard landscape, I planted a row of Hill's weeping fig; eventually these will be pleached. Both the swimming pool on three sides and the retaining walls between the two terraces are framed in box hedging. Box, lonicera and weeping fig trees, with some wisteria on the house wall – that really was the only planting needed to create a green courtyard.

THIS BACK COURTYARD proves that space restriction doesn't mean the drama has to be underplayed (opposite page). The basic elements of terracing, planting and fountain are restrained; it is their scale – and the considerable presence of the pair of sphinxes – that makes the garden so impressive.

The front avenue of tilias seems in perfect proportion to the house, but was only made possible because the house was set so far back on its block (previous pages). Gravel as pure as snow completed the European look of house and garden.

THIS TRADITIONAL 1930s house exudes the confidence that comes from long occupancy of a site and solid construction. By the time I arrived to refurbish the garden, the house was well settled into its (considerable) grounds.

The front garden contained a perfect loop of carriageway, leaving a balance of encircling flowerbeds and central lawn. My task, as I saw it, was simply to devise a new planting scheme for the existing beds and to soften the house, which the carriageway had left quite exposed. To achieve the latter aim I first added an ornamental pool in the middle of the circular lawn, with a coping painted white to match the house and one jet. Balls of English box added on either side of the portico were matched by balls of box at four corners of the eight-sided pool so that the house seems to step into the garden. Small hedges of box, planted against the house's façade, and *Erigeron karvinskianus* around the pool further counteracted the hard surfaces of wall and gravel carriageway. But still the house looked exposed. The space was there so I planted a pair of pin oaks (*Quercus palustris*) on the lawn to frame both fountain and portico. In time they will grow quite large, but the house can take it. Behind the fence on the street boundary I planted a hedge of clipped lillypilly, and in the deep corners of the flowerbeds massed *Gardenia augusta* 'Florida' and *Viburnum plicatum* – a very white and green scheme in keeping with house and lawn.

The back garden contained a tennis court against the far boundary and a big swimming pool between the court and the house, both of which the owners wished to preserve. Accordingly the court was resurfaced, and the pool relined in green tiles. There was no point trying to hide the dominant pool; it became a matter of giving it an ornamental as well as a practical function, and of integrating it with its setting (see pages 60–1). We surrounded it with handsome bluestone pavers to match the substantial terrace we had built adjacent to the

house – and to tone with the house's lichen-covered terracotta roof tiles. The pool also gained a bullnose coping of bluestone.

A see-through safety fence demonstrated that the swimming pool was part of the garden; a trimmed line of box on the house side of the glass did the actual work of connecting the swimming pool to the garden. Deep flowerbeds at either end of the pool area, with a *Tilia cordata* tree at each corner, and *Hydrangea paniculata*, *H. arborescens*, *Alchemilla mollis* and erigeron planted below, completed the process.

A medium hedge of *Viburnum odoratissimum* that flowers beautifully was planted between the pool and the tennis court. The far fence, painted dark green to fudge the boundary, took a taller row of Manchurian pear trees. The foreshortened view from the house terrace is now of lower hedge against higher one, with little suggestion of a tennis court between.

The rest of the back garden was designed with children in mind: essentially it became a big lawn around a wonderful, National-Trust-classified hornbeam of a size to offset the house itself. In a part of the garden that had been bulldozed to rationalise the layout, there had stood a structure that repeated the white brickwork and roof tiles of the house. I was struck by the concept and took photos before it came down. Bringing to the garden the solidity and style of the house – in the form of several masonry structures – seemed the key to keeping the garden in both proportion and relationship with the house. What resulted were two substantial gateways, capped with old tiles, leading into the tennis-court area, one allowing entry from the pool enclosure (see page 61), the other from lawn flanked by flowerbeds further to one side (see pages 62–3). On the adjacent side wall a fountain-back in the same style was built, with a spout that spills water into a pool reminiscent of, though simpler than, the pool in the front garden.

THE THIRD OF THREE

gateways was given a blind arch to support a spout from which water flows to a semicircular pool, edged with erigeron (above). Two attached coach lamps light the fountain.

The second white wooden gate into the tennis court, like the first one in the swimming-pool enclosure, forms a porthole with the gateway arch, through which a Manchurian pear tree may be glimpsed.

THE OWNER OF the back garden shown in the next pages wanted to include an outdoor dining area; wanted the existing swimming pool to be more ornamental; and wanted to have more privacy. As well, it was obvious that any design would need to take into account the scale of the imposing Edwardian house and the building material, red brick – and get the colours right. The original house was one storey but built on a slope steep enough for the owner to have recently added a separate recreation area underneath; this opens into the garden so that became a factor also.

To achieve privacy and block out the tall houses on three sides, we planted my favourite pleached Manchurian pear trees at intervals of about 2.5 metres. The Manchurian pears have proved a particularly successful choice. The root system is not highly invasive – an essential factor with trees close to swimming pools and walls – and does not use up all the nutrients and water in the soil. And the trees' brief dormant period coincides with winter when the swimming pool is not in use. The hedge they have formed needs clipping only twice a year to keep it to a height of 4 or 5 metres: if the trees were allowed to grow to their full height, their lower branches would be too high to screen neighbouring buildings. The trees filter but do not totally block out light so Trachelospermum asiaticum, employed here as usual as a border, and the azalea 'Alba Magnifica' thrive below them in the 2-metre-wide beds the garden permits. To create a three-layered effect these plants too are clipped – which doesn't prevent the azaleas' delicate white blooms from appearing in spring or the climber's fragrant white flowers in summer.

In developing the design I was constrained by the position of the swimming pool (to one side, towards the back of the property); by the existing two terraces, the lower of which was tied to the swimming pool; and by the need, given the garden's proposed uses, to pave most of the ground surface. On the other hand the size and shape of the area (roughly 20 metres by 20 metres) offered considerable scope for design.

I decided to divide it widthwise, adding greatly to its interest and alleviating the visual power of the paving and the pool. Two low planter boxes were constructed as dividers (see pages 66–7). They part at the centre to create a wide break of about 7 metres. The half of the divided garden nearer the house became a terrace accessing the driveway to one side as well as the house. It also became the new outdoor dining area. Beyond the planter boxes, and one step down, the second terrace remained the swimming-pool area.

The planter boxes were constructed in red brick to extend the main building material to the garden. To meet the strength of the red brick, deep terracotta-coloured pavers were chosen and the pool was renovated with dark blue tiles. The garden began to take on something of a bright resort feeling. This I enhanced with the planting not only of the rather lush side beds, but also of clipped lillypilly hedges in the planter boxes: where these boxes end in two square piers that mark the central opening, spiky cycads (my favourite Cycas revoluta) add a suggestion of palms – without taking up the room that palms would.

In addition to deciding on new tiles, I redesigned the pool to give it straight sides, although I kept both it and the poolside area quite large still, in scale with the house. Straightening the lines allowed me to install an ornamental pool at one end, against a backdrop of garden bed. The design works well. The open space between the two planter boxes prevents either terrace from seeming too constricted, yet the outdoor dining and swimming-pool areas are kept comfortably separate. The swimming pool no longer dominates the whole back garden, but is just one part of it.

A FINE BRONZE URN, *mounted on a plinth in the centre of the new ornamental pool, was converted to a fountain (opposite page). The lustre of the bronze brings out the blue of the adjacent swimming pool and the terracotta of the new paving. Fish flitting between water lilies add their flashes of gold.*

IN AUTUMN THE LEAVES

of the Manchurian pear trees that form
the background to the whole garden add
to the rich tones of terracotta pavers and
red-brick walls; the evergreen foundation
of Trachelospermum asiaticum, *clipped
azaleas, lillypilly and palm-like cycads
provides a necessary counterpoise (above).*

*Not just people relaxing on the lower
terrace enjoy the bronze urn shown on
page 65, which was placed in a small
pond at one end of the swimming pool to
give the area a decorative, not solely a
functional, purpose. Those sitting at the
dining table to one side of the upper
terrace look through the opening and
across the blue water of the larger pool
to the falling water of the smaller one.*

THIS URBAN BACK garden offered a rare opportunity to meet all the owners' requests – for a dining terrace, for a lawn on which children could play, for a swimming pool and for a tennis court – without having to force the design. Giving all these parts of the garden generous proportions was imperative to visually balance the imposing double-storey house and anchor it within its garden.

The area was approximately 30 metres by 40 metres: sufficiently wide to allow the north–south tennis court to run across the back boundary (and slightly out of sight on one side because of the odd shape of the block). This meant that the back garden automatically fell into two roughly equal parts, with enough room for the remaining half to be on two levels: a lower, grassed one in front of the tennis court, in which a swimming pool could be built to one side; and an upper, dining terrace, wrapping around the L-shaped house and accessed by the centrally located back door.

Part of the owners' brief was that the tennis court must look as if it was not a tennis court. The solution I chose – to disguise the court – was similar to the one I arrived at when designing the tennis court of the 1930s house shown on pages 58–63, but the means chosen were rather different and had to do with the different character of the two houses.

Firstly the court was subtly separated from the rest of the garden by the erection of a chinoiserie latticework pavilion and soft plantings. Secondly the block's dominant east–west axis – which runs not merely from the back door down the middle of the garden, but actually from the front door of the house – was emphasised in such a way as to distract attention from the tennis court. From the house the eye takes in the amplitude of the dining terrace yet is strongly directed beyond, along this main axis: retaining walls on the upper level part

sufficiently to allow two steps to descend to paired pavers, which cross the lower lawn. These pavers carry the eye – and the main traffic – from the house to the pavilion. (Made of white sandstone, the 500-millimetre by 500-millimetre pavers match the 600-millimetre by 600-millimetre ones used on the dining terrace and mark the transition from a passive to an active area of the garden.)

The main axis, however, was not allowed to culminate at the pavilion, arresting though it is, but at the back boundary, on the far side of the tennis court, where a 2.5-metre-high urn on a pedestal was positioned. By placing the final elaboration of the axis at the extreme end of the property, vista after vista was opened up – an *enfilade* created.

The urn was tucked into a tall hedge so that it in no way sat baldly beside the tennis court; however, this hedge and those flanking the other fences have the usual primary purpose of blocking out neighbouring houses. The bulk of the 4-metre-high evergreen hedging became Leyland cypress (x *Cupressocyparis leylandii*), with a side hedge of aromatic bay (*Laurus nobilis*) close to the house.

It's a special occasion when a pavilion can be designed. Pavilions are pleasure places meant for the viewing of delightful garden vistas; part of a dream of a perfect summer's day. They need space and careful siting both to offer a vantage point and be seen to advantage, and most urban blocks are just too small. But pavilions also require a certain kind of garden. The owners of this one are English and they wanted an English country garden to complement their Georgian-style house: lots of roses, irises and lavenders; a heavy emphasis on spring and summer flowering; soft pinks, blues, mauves, whites, yellows and greens, with here and there richer pinks and even a splash of crimson, but nothing that

EVERY ELEMENT IN *the back garden was organised to carry the eye from the house and the upper dining terrace to a large elevated urn, framed by a latticework pavilion (opposite page). The urn actually stands on the far side of the disguised tennis court.*

clashed. The soft furnishings inside the house are chintz so the planting extended those flowers and colours outside to deep flowerbeds on the upper and lower terraces and separating the tennis court from the lawn of the lower one. In winter this very seasonal garden draws on the lines of the pavilion and the other external structures for its strength, and on the evergreen hedges.

From the pavilion the garden stretches in all directions. Afternoon tea can be taken on a wrought-iron table and the tennis or the swimming observed. A rose-draped wooden frame, open to the garden except for panels of chinoiserie latticework matching those of the pavilion, was extended on either side to form a graceful barrier between the garden and the tennis court. Strong features such as pavilions aren't good set starkly on their own – they look far too awkward – so the tall frame added to tie this pavilion to the sides of the garden served a dual aesthetic purpose. The white paint of these structures took its cue from the white trim of the house. The artificial grass of the tennis court, glimpsed through the roses and the latticework, reads as an extension of the lawn.

The swimming pool was hidden from the dining terrace by the higher, right-hand wing of the retaining walls. I wanted it to look more like an ornamental pond than a swimming pool so it was set straight into the lawn with just an edging of the house bricks, and its interior was painted green to match the green of the lawn. Lawn and water seem to flow into each other.

There was sufficient space to the left of the tennis court for the owners to have a picking garden, but to get to it a side walk was needed. I decided to train *Laburnum* x *watereri* 'Vossii' over a series of metal arches; in spring

THE UPPER TERRACE ON
the left-hand side gives views down a laburnum-laden tunnel and across the lawn of the lower terrace to the chinoiserie pavilion and the sunken swimming pool.

it becomes an overwhelming tunnel of pendant yellow racemes. The walk itself was constructed of bricks laid on edge in diamonds, with loose gravel between. This secondary east–west axis added complexity to the garden, yet as is so often the case it was born from practical need.

Even though the block is large, secondary ornamentation was kept restrained – nothing was to detract from the pavilion and the central raised urn. The dining terrace looks across some lawn on the right to a bed of shade-loving plants in front of the bay hedge, at the centre of which was positioned a simple fountain with a brick trough capped in sandstone. All hard finishes chosen for the garden referred back to the architecture of the house: they were made either brick to match the walls or sandstone to match the mouldings. The piers of all retaining walls were topped with sandstone spheres – their shape echoed in the living balls of English box grown to mark the entries to the laburnum walk. Two robust lemon trees in large tubs were placed symmetrically to emphasise the wide entry to the pavilion: artificial ornamentation would have spoilt the airy look of that structure and been out of keeping with the wooden latticework. Finally light wrought-iron furniture was placed on the dining terrace to augment, not impede, the effect of an *enfilade*.

THE LABURNUM WALK
consists of gravel, with a crisscross pattern in red brick, and is edged with low hedges of box (opposite page). A pair of sandstone spheres tops the sandstone-capped piers at the entry from the upper terrace.

Balls of box, repeating the shape of the sandstone spheres employed on the piers of the retaining walls, decorate the entry from the lower terrace to the laburnum walk, while maintaining the 'naturalness' of the flowerbeds and lawn (previous pages).

Even though the block is large, secondary ornamentation was kept restrained – nothing was to detract from the pavilion and the central raised urn.

OCCASIONALLY a garden has to wait for the final touch that completes the balance of elements in its design. Five or so years ago I built the front garden shown on the opposite page, which featured in my book *The Boxed Garden*. In that book I described how I had created a large Moorish-influenced wall fountain to match the imposing Spanish Mission style house. Water fell from a bronze lotus, specially forged for the fountain, onto a snake-entwined Indian lingam, found in an antique shop, and finally into a plain, bow-fronted pool built on site. The lotus was mounted on an equally plain fountain-back consisting of a blind arch inset with white pebbles.

Although the fountain is framed by the handsome iron gate through which people enter the garden, at the time I wanted to direct the eye to it further by adding a low water channel, or rill. But the owners were uncertain about the concept so I didn't pursue it. Some time later, however, they visited the Alhambra in southern Spain and saw how magically water is moved in that supremely Moorish garden. The upshot was that they asked me to complete the original design by running a narrow, shallow channel across the lawn from the fountain. The channel was lined, and paved on either side, with the pale pavers that had been used throughout the garden. To add to the fascination of moving water, I laid squares of the green pebbles used elsewhere in the garden, in bands 300 millimetres apart, down the middle of the rill.

BALANCE FROM ELABORATION: *the water channel recently added to this Moorish front garden is fed by water that flows from the original pool of the fountain into a new, lower pool, bringing an extra dimension to the ornamental water of the garden (opposite page).*

A QUITE DIFFERENT front garden and fountain are shown on the following pages. The garden belongs to a townhouse designed by the architect Wayne Gillespie, who died quite recently.

A carriageway enters and exits at either end of the front wall, leaving a scoop of garden facing the front door. Given the shape and the space limitations of this segment, a saucer with a single spurt of water seemed the most appropriate way to establish the major sight-line from front door to front wall without compromising the integrity of the house's strongly contemporary design. The bowl reinforced the only soft lines – the elliptical curve of the drive – in a built environment that was otherwise all straight lines.

To make the play of water more interesting loose, brown pebbles were placed within the saucer; the same pebbles, set in concrete, formed the surface of the carriageway. The fountain needed to be framed by an equally simple massed planting – a background of the tall evergreen shrub *Viburnum odoratissimum*, clipped to a height of about 2.5 metres, and a carpet of *Trachelospermum asiaticum*.

BALANCE FROM SIMPLICITY: *a single jet of water, uplit at night, is sufficient to provide focus in a minimalist front garden (following pages).*

A PAIR OF NEW townhouses in an inner suburb provided an excellent opportunity to achieve a balanced design because I worked with the architect and the owners from the start. Working together meant that all the important considerations – the use of spaces, the treatment of levels, the placement of windows in relation to the garden – could be approached logically. The townhouses are restrained, rather neutral, which suits their urban setting and the limited space. The architect is well known for this style and for his sense of symmetry. I think the owners recognised our work would be compatible.

Being able to integrate building and garden was a great satisfaction, but it did not mean that the garden areas of both townhouses were easy to design. Typically they consist of three small spaces: a front area meant purely to make people feel welcome when they arrive; a rear courtyard, envisaged as a paved entertainment and play area combined; and a long, narrow sideway connecting the two, which is viewed from various rooms.

The front of the townhouse shown opposite is restricted not only in terms of space but also in terms of soil because of an underground garage, entered from the street on one side of the block. And, since the house is quite elevated above the street, recessed steps eat into the space. Consequently every surface became important – yet most needed to be hard, and that introduced the danger that the house might seem uninviting. This was overcome by seizing every possibility to plant.

The riser of each recessed step was given the merest strip of *Lonicera nitida*. At night, when lit, the steps make quite an entrancing approach to the house. A tiny strip of lonicera also lines a very narrow bed at the foot of the front wall on the street side. Behind it rises a second tier of greenery – actually just Boston ivy climbing up (and over) the wall. I find Boston ivy or climbing

fig particularly good in these situations – and they stop graffiti. They only need a 200-millimetre-wide bed, although the wall footings must be 300–400 millimetres below ground to leave room for the planting.

Only one bed could be created in the front garden, and it had to be set against the front wall, the sole part where earth had been retained. The bed (only about 2 metres by 4 metres) was composed of two squares of lonicera, each divided into four triangles by lines of English box, clipped a little higher than the lonicera. (The triangle nearest the steps was not in fact lonicera but gravel to give the entry sufficient amplitude.) I preferred to keep the bed green on green rather than fill the compartments with another colour. In such a small garden sufficient colour is provided already by the off-white rendered house and garden walls, the similarly toned pavers I chose and the wrought-iron gate, selected with care by the owners and allowed to rust to a compatible colour. However, orange trees placed in terracotta pots, lime-washed to match the house, at the centre of both squares – all the decoration the small space could take – do bear fruit, and in autumn the Boston ivy changes colour, so the planting is not completely monochromatic.

For people who wish to sit for a moment in this enclosed front garden and contemplate the simple parterre, we popped a wooden seat against the boundary wall that continues along the sideway. Lines of star jasmine (*Trachelospermum jasminoides*) were trained on steel wires to crisscross the entire length of this wall, linking the front and back garden.

The cement pavers used in the front were continued throughout the garden. In the front, however, they were laid in a plain grid – as I think any paved area of less than 2 or 3 metres in width should be. A pattern of pebble inserts (like one I was to design for the back garden of the second townhouse to break up the blandness

A RIBBON OF LOW HEDGING is an element I frequently use to soften the hard interface between house façade and paving (opposite page). The Boston ivy employed here was particularly necessary in a front garden where an underground garage and recessed steps from the street restricted the planting area.

there) would only have emphasised the smallness of the space. Besides, they were not necessary here: the planting patterns were enough.

Although similar hard and soft materials were used for the gardens of both townhouses, the designs differed except for their sideways, and it is the sideway of the second townhouse that is shown here. It is very narrow, less than 2 metres in width, so even an ingeniously designed fountain such as the one in the sideway shown on page 29 was not an option. The path would have to be a minimum of 1–1.2 metres, and what space there was left over would have to be concreted because the sideway, like much of the front garden, is over the garage. Any 'garden' would have to be a planter box, filled to a depth of about 300 millimetres with soil.

The crisscrossing star jasmine was the solution and left just enough room in the paver-faced planter for a hedge of box; neither of these plants requires much soil, but they do of course need very regular feeding because soil nutrients are quickly depleted in this kind of environment.

The vibrant star jasmine makes the 2-metre-wide crisscrosses appear strikingly three-dimensional, although in fact they take up little space. Because the sideway is so long and narrow, and because major rooms look onto it, consistency of planting seemed all-important. As people move from room to room, bold crosses beyond the windows – and the summery fragrance of jasmine – travel with them.

As well as catering for general traffic, this sideway had to provide water play! Since there was not sufficient room at the back for a swimming pool, the owners asked for an outdoor shower that their children could romp under in summer. I decided to set paver stepping stones in loose pebbles through which the water (and rainwater) could percolate, to be carried away by drains in the concrete slab. I used quite large (40-millimetre) pebbles, making sure that they were smooth enough for small, bare feet. The chunkiness adds interest to the surface, but also ensures they do not get carried inside on feet or shoes to scratch the polished-wood floors.

BOLD CRISSCROSSES OF
star jasmine that seem to have a lusty
life of their own were used to exploit the
length of the side wall since there was no
way of playing it down. A showerhead lets
children frolic under water in summer.

OFTEN A DESIGN is influenced by how much time can be spent maintaining the garden. The owners of this Sydney garden had retired; they wanted a very formal, very clipped garden and were happy to put in the hours of maintenance themselves to keep it immaculate. That gave me licence to have lots of controlled hedges, lots of topiary. The house lent itself to that kind of formality. However, the oceanside property is subject to strong salt winds so not many types of plants were going to do well there.

The front garden is wide (about 18 metres) but shallow (only about 10 metres), and even that depth varies because of a massive porticoed bay window protruding into the garden. The success of the design devised resides largely in its foundation of planting, based on tiering and an interplay of greens. A line of Hill's weeping fig trees were stood to attention along the front wall. The trees have been clipped into individual squares at wall height, although I am now recommending that the owners let them join together to further protect the other plants — the wind really can howl around this garden. Murraya hedges border a flowerbed on one side of the garden and separate the garden from the front path on the other. Japanese box (*Buxus microphylla* var. *japonica*) has been trimmed into balls to elaborate both ends of these hedges: Japanese box does much better in Sydney than English box.

In the interests of the garden's disciplined design,

the owners were happy to limit flowering plants to white *Gardenia augusta* 'Florida', planted in the 1.5-metre-wide by 3-metre-long side bed of the garden. All through summer the garden is filled with the overwhelming perfume of the gardenias, which flower extravagantly in the moist heat.

Alternating squares of thyme (*Thymus vulgaris*) and pavers were set in fine, sepia-coloured gravel adjacent to the house's façade. The thyme was a way of extending soft green to the horizontal plane in a garden where an imposing house needed to be offset by a proportionately large paved and gravelled area.

The main focus of the front garden became a long ornamental pool, sited so that it was the central view from the sitting room: a low pool, surrounded by a murraya hedge grown to just below the plain coping (a height of less than 300 millimetres). At its centre was placed a statue rather than a fountain. At my suggestion the owners quite carefully considered the form and face of several before making a final choice of a squatting boy — after all, they would be looking at the statue whenever they glanced up from the sitting room or worked in the garden. The placement of the statue represents a rare case where I have been happy to decidedly underscale, not overscale, a feature. It works because of the reeds grown around it, which add verticality. The viewer feels drawn down into the heart of the garden, away from the blustery world beyond it.

A DOMINANT SEMICIRCULAR *bay window (not seen in the photograph), with a portico, is balanced by 'bands' of paving, rectangular ornamental pool, and square-topped weeping fig trees (opposite page). The interplay of pavers and squares of thyme set in gravel, the varied use of hedging for definition and the soft side bed of massed gardenias ensure that these bands are not themselves too heavy for the space.*

OCCASIONALLY a town garden needs no problems solved, requires no compromises and offers the designer ample space to play with. This was one such garden. The new house and the garden were planned at the same time and the house the architect designed was well sited on the large block of land, with a generous 12 metres by 40 metres approximately left in front. The formality of the house suited my style of design and the space gave me free rein.

The front had to be foremost an appropriately grand approach for a rather grand house; everything about it had to herald the fine portico and main door. I began with a layered planting on the street boundary. Boston ivy now covers the front retaining wall on the side facing the tree-lined street. In front of the wrought-iron front fence, above the Boston ivy, is a hedge of English box; behind the front fence, a higher hedge of lillypilly.

Visitors from the street climb steps that rise between these tiers of green to handsome wrought-iron gates. Once inside the gates they find themselves in a broad, paved forecourt with before them a large fountain, and beyond that the house. At the fountain the paving divides to go around it; as it does, paths lead off to wings of garden left and right. Visitors must take in the fountain and glimpse the garden wings before they can arrive at the front door.

Because of the luxury of space, the shape of the fountain's ornamental pool could be quite elaborate. The design is a traditional Islamic motif of a square, 2 metres by 2 metres, with a scallop on each side, set within a square cross formed by box hedging. Since all visitors must go past the fountain, I chose a shape that would appear easy to move around despite its corners. The fountain itself consists of jets of water set at the four points of the pool, on its broad lip; water arcs inwards to a column of water rising from a fifth jet at the centre

of the pool. The water display is even more spectacular at night, when each jet is uplit. The water feature seems fittingly impressive, yet the detail is actually quite minimal: simple box edging, simple water jets. No cavorting carved figures or entwined dolphins or ascending stone bowls, for nothing could be allowed to block out the house's lovely entrance and spoil the climax of the walk.

Hornbeams, planted in box-edged beds about 1.8 metres wide, formed the basis of the garden's identical wings, one step up from the forecourt. (Even this garden is not without tall neighbouring buildings that need to be hidden.) The 4-metre-high hornbeams give the whole garden enormous dignity, their own mass helping to anchor the heavy masonry of the house. The rest is just gravel with paver stepping stones so that visitors feel free to enter the wings — in warmer months to be delightfully surprised by pale pink and white roses reaching out from between the hornbeams. The owners love this flower so the front was organised to double as a rose garden, while never relying on these plants for its year-round impact. The front garden is essentially European in that it is seasonal. There are the flowering of roses in spring, with an autumn flush as well; the rich autumn foliage of the hornbeams and the Boston ivy; and the tracery of bare hornbeam branches in winter.

Matching stone urns, raised about 1.6 metres and placed at the end of each wing, draw visitors further inside and elongate the secondary axis (see pages 90–1). Positioned where they are, the urns in no way compete for attention with the central water feature.

Most of the pleasure of the front garden design comes from its unity of scale, its correct proportions, and above all its unforced formality. Like the house, it extensively borrows design elements from the European tradition and is quite true to that tradition, I think. But it

THE OWNERS ADDED

a nineteenth-century Coalbrook cast-iron seat at the entry to both wings of the front garden to take advantage of the view of the forecourt's central fountain.

At the back the house seems built on water, broad stairs descending through the scent of gardenias to the swimming pool (following pages). A pergola swagged in wisteria and bordered by a hedge of Prunus lusitanica *simultaneously hides the empty space of the tennis court and opens a series of 'windows' to pear trees on the boundaries.*

is still an Australian garden for the twenty-first century: not only because of its simplicity, for the formal style has often been employed simply, but because it relates to the way we live now – in an urban environment and with an urban need for even grand gardens to be unfussy and easily cared for.

The atmosphere of the back garden is quite different from that of the front, although just as much created by the interaction of house and garden. The owners wanted a feeling of the resorts they enjoy so much in the south of France. To capture this, I designed a huge swimming pool – it takes up perhaps half of an area measuring 16 metres by 16 metres – adjacent to the house. People flow out the French doors of the house onto a broad terrace designed to be large enough to take several groupings of chairs and sun lounges under market umbrellas. Before them wide steps lead down to blue water. The effect of a grand descent (although it consists of only four steps) was achieved by cutting the steps into the terrace and turning the large squares of terrace remaining at either end into 'hanging gardens' filled with Gardenia augusta 'Florida'. The gardenias, tall urns from which annuals spill in summertime, and festoons of wisteria bring a sense of lushness to an area that in reality is mainly pool and paving.

The owners wanted a spa large enough to take lots of people. This was not something that could be placed inconspicuously so I positioned it directly opposite the steps, framed by two columns of a pergola on the far side and elevated sufficiently for a sheet of water to fall to the pool below. In this way the spa looks part of an integrated design; in scale with its surroundings; and, most important of all, a water feature of sufficient presence to be a true focus for the terrace.

THE BACK GARDEN IS *heavy with lighting: not just because the terrace, swimming pool and spa are used on summer nights, but because all the main living rooms look into it (opposite page). The pool and steps are lit; the pergola, spa and spilling water are lit; the urns are lit. The wisteria is uplit.*

It relates to the way we live now – in an urban environment and with an urban need for even grand gardens to be unfussy and easily cared for.

THE KEY to designing the huge back garden shown in the following pages was to scale all the elements accordingly. Everything was huge: the renovated old two-storey house; the 70-year-old trees framing the garden; the pavilion recently constructed as an entry to the tennis court at the far end of the otherwise derelict garden. The logic was clearly to utilise the axis running from the central French doors of the house to the pavilion. Near to the house, along this axis, I placed an 'avenue' of orange trees in six oversized, wooden 'Versailles' planter boxes, on either side of paired stepping stones, which gave way to a stretch of lawn. A 20-metre by 5-metre lily pond, as big as a swimming pool, set flush with the lawn, completed the definition of the sight-line. To enhance the traditional, long-established feel of the back garden, rhododendrons, azaleas and a host of shade-loving perennials were planted in generous, 5-metre-wide beds under the old trees and under the new row of pleached Hill's weeping fig trees, introduced on either side of the pavilion to screen the tennis court. This uncluttered design demonstrates, I think, that space to spare doesn't mean the layout should necessarily be complex. Here it was more important to match the character and scale of the house and its remnant garden.

THE WATER FEATURE WAS

kept as restrained as the rest of the back garden: six jets set in a line down the middle of the immensely long lily pond were sufficient for a display.

The view along the central axis from the tennis pavilion: in the distance two clipped English box hedges part to direct the eye to the central French doors of the house (following pages). They also mark a change of level down to the house terrace, with its 'avenue' of orange trees in planter boxes.

97

A GARDEN vying for attention with its house always looks unbalanced, always jars. This front garden is simple because the façade of the house, influenced by those of houses in French towns, is quite elaborate. Two antique Anduze pots were chosen as the main adornment of a terrace built adjacent to the front door, to continue the French connection. Other than that the garden was conceived as a sea of gravel, again in the French manner, with banks of *Hydrangea macrophylla* 'Blue Wave' planted in front of stone boundary walls constructed to match the carved sandstone of the façade.

These walls were built quite high, but not so high that the garden couldn't borrow an upper storey from the huge pin oaks lining the street beyond.

The Anduze pots had drainage holes drilled in them so that they could be watered by, and drain into, pipes set in the concrete slab when the terrace was built. This prevents the pots from weeping mucky water onto the surrounding pale pavers – a common hazard with pots. The pots stand a metre high – 1.6 metres when the topiary cones of English box are included. The two pots anchor the garden, and add a lustre while in no way competing with the façade.

A MASSED PLANTING OF Hydrangea macrophylla *'Blue Wave'* enlivens the courtyard without hiding the fine stone walls of the garden (above left).

Reproduction Anduze pots are slightly sandblasted to make their glaze seem worn, but these two antique pots have the true patina of age (opposite page). Oxides in the coats of glazing have streaked the pots green and brown over the years.

CREATING A CHANGE of level, even if it results in little more than a raised ledge, always helps overcome the problem of imbalance in a limited space that has large demands made on it. In this L-shaped back courtyard, elevating the garden on the far side of the swimming pool produced what was essentially only a long planter box (see pages 104–5), but into that could be tucked three layers of planting: miniature agapanthus, orange trees, and Manchurian pear trees allowed to grow 5 or 6 metres high but clipped to only a metre wide.

A large, centrally placed wall fountain, its water trickling from a bronze spout to a bronze bowl and then to a raised pond and finally the swimming pool itself, was tucked in also. Wider and higher planter boxes, out of the way of terrace traffic, were possible at the two ends of the elevated back bed; these in their turn made possible the planting of two *Phoenix canariensis* palms.

The result, I think, is a sense of luxuriance that fulfils the owners' desire for a garden reminiscent of the ones they love in the south of France, without any corresponding sense that the layout has been strained to achieve that effect.

SITTING-ROOM WINDOWS
*look across to a wall fountain in the side part of the L-shaped back courtyard. This fountain, like the central one in the main section of the garden, is part of a raised bed and set against a backing of inset pebbles, but here a graceful female figure spills water into a bow-fronted trough filled with water irises (*Iris kaempferi*).*

The swimming pool in the main part is no more than a lap pool but widens, opposite its fountain, to allow for recessed steps (following pages). To further ensure the pool did not look squeezed into too small a space, the terrace's artificial-stone pavers were repeated on its surfaces and steps. It's not a pool meant for water bombing, but rather for grown-ups to sit on the steps talking!

I DON'T OFTEN design commercial gardens, but they're very much a part of city life and in many ways the principles that apply to private gardens apply to them. Certainly the CEO of the company whose premises are shown here wanted a garden with the feel of an intimate domestic courtyard into which the offices could look and in which customers and employees could be entertained. However, any commercial site obviously requires particularly hardy plants and low-maintenance grounds. There was plenty of space in the 25-metre by 25-metre area, bounded on three sides by the building and on the fourth by the car park, to plant two rows of four Manchurian pear trees and allow them to grow to their full height and width without pruning, and also two Chinese elms at the car park entrance.

The rows of pear trees are perfectly balanced by a substantial (10-metre by 3-metre) rectangular pool placed between them. The suitably plain pool is just outlined by a slightly higher hedge of English box, repeating the planting chosen to form the large 'cushions' on which the pear trees appear to rest. The box needs to be trimmed only two times a year. (Elsewhere ivy – perhaps the toughest plant of all – is used as a neat, weed-smothering ground cover.)

The pavers and pool are grey, the pool coating black, to harmonise with the building materials of the rather imposing offices. The colours are severe and the planting minimal, but the pear trees, left to flourish in their natural form, ensure the space is soft and harmonious for users and onlookers.

JETS OF WATER

are projected inwards from the long sides to the centre of the ornamental pool in these commercial premises. The garden created is large scale like the building; very simple like the building; very clean-lined like the building.

THIS COURTYARD, onto which the kitchen and a small dining area give, is just one part of a very large Sydney harbourside property on three levels. The owner wanted a picking garden that would provide herbs for the kitchen, and a place where she could spell house plants for a while.

I designed a long flowerbed to extend along the two boundaries and to face the house windows across an expanse of paving on which a table and chairs could be set. The bed was edged with, and divided at the far end into compartments by, murraya, clipped to a height of 300 millimetres. As other gardens in the book have shown, it is one of the plants I often choose for hedging in Sydney to replace the English box I use in more temperate climates. The murraya grows faster than box, but needs pruning more regularly. I use it primarily for its dense, green foliage – if its small, fragrant flowers are wanted, then it mustn't be clipped so heavily.

The centrepiece of the longer side of the bed is a lovely freestanding sandstone fountain placed against the existing wall. Imported from France, the fountain takes the form of a classical head from which water spouts into a trough below. On either side of it I planted two spectacular *Magnolia grandiflora*, which also love humid heat. Like all the other plants chosen for this garden, they tolerate salty air. They were planted as fairly advanced trees, specifically to hide a dominating house close by. However, there was a danger with such large evergreens that they would take over the courtyard and hide the harbour view so their branches are very regularly pruned to restrain their spread – this does not inhibit their flowering. (As long as *M. grandiflora* is kept trimmed, its roots tend not to be a problem, although the root system of any tree, but particularly evergreens, is always a potential threat to nearby hard surfaces.) The owner puts her recuperating house plants in the shade of the magnolias, and plants her herbs and picking flowers in the compartments at the far end of the bed in full sun.

The owner and I agreed that the courtyard should convey an overwhelming feeling of greenery so between the pavers were planted native violets (*Viola hederacea*). The violets have been very successful because the courtyard offers the shade they need. The pavers are quite large (500 millimetres by 500 millimetres) to make it easy for people to walk around without bruising the plants.

CHAIRS ARE BROUGHT OUT
so that people can relax in this garden and enjoy the pleasures of water – wide harbour views and water trickling from a fountain (opposite page).

IF THIS BOOK'S selection of town gardens has demonstrated anything, it is that balance has to be worked at even on the occasions when there's space to play with. Yet every now and then a solution is so easy that it takes you by surprise. This house has a long indoor swimming pool giving onto, through a series of glass doors, an equally long colonnade. The sphere-topped square pillars of the colonnade were quite overpowering until innocuous ribbons of wisteria were twined around them. Suddenly the earth-bound weight of the inanimate pillars was counteracted by the spiralling green life of the wisteria. Small squares of English box to alleviate the harsh juncture of columns and paving seem to carry the colonnade triumphantly into the garden.

When something like this happens I know why, despite all the frustrations of working with imperfect conditions and changeable plants, I love to design gardens.

THE JAUNTY MAYPOLES
that the pillars of the colonnade have
become rise out of amusingly minute
boxes of trimmed hedge.

110

COUNTRY

Scale is the dramatic thing about a country garden. There is so much space and so much that can be done with it. Vistas and focal points, garden rooms and generous proportions, all those kinds of wonderful elements come into play. The country gives you great flexibility, great opportunity to achieve a balanced garden. You are free of the constraints of boundaries, and noise, and neighbours overlooking the garden. The only trap is clinging to a city sense of scale, making paths and drives too narrow, terraces too small.

Yet the country is not a protected environment. Its gardens are open to heat and drought, strong winds, heavy frosts, even snow. The aspect of a property needs to be right, the climate amenable, the soil suitable, good access and adequate water available. In hilly terrain is the land on the sunny or the shady side? The rainy or the rain-shadow side? Is it sheltered? Or is it facing into rough or salty winds?

Steps lead up from the crab-apple walk to the main courtyard of a Margaret River garden (page 113). The garden is featured on pages 124–31.

The east room of the garden at St Ambrose Farm: the bays of the northern section are not visible from the first part of the room, but must be discovered by the visitor (previous pages). St Ambrose Farm is described on pages 136–43.

City gardeners work within some climatic constraints, but a reliable water supply and an addition of topsoil usually solve the other main problems. In the country the limitations of terrain and weather are not so easily overcome. The cost of putting in a dam or bringing in endless loads of topsoil is considerable. You need to understand the climate and soil and work with them, not against them; to do careful preliminary research on suitable plants; to experiment over several years with specimens and grow only what thrives. You have to be quite disciplined otherwise costs will be prohibitive. Even in the country you can never have everything you want.

In any case a good design in terms of the country is never one developed with reference only to personal desires. The garden should always be at home within the wider setting. The twentieth-century English designer Russell Page, whose work I greatly admire, believed deeply in the 'genius of the place'. For him that meant taking his cue from the surrounding landscape; from the views, the climate, the nature of the vegetation, the topography, the materials and colours of the location.

Understanding from the start that the house is part of the garden has huge implications in the country: on a large piece of land so much is gained by both if a new house is properly sited, so much opportunity lost if it is not. In the country the designer has the chance, not offered by city gardens, to be a 'place maker' or 'site maker'. The supreme place maker was Capability Brown, who built complete landscapes for great houses in eighteenth-century England: if he wanted a house altered to suit his garden design, his instructions were followed; if he wanted a small hill, earth was moved; if he wanted a lake, a stream was dammed; if he wanted a forest, huge trees were transplanted. Hardly practical these days! Nevertheless a degree of earth moving is usually involved in the establishment of a large country garden. Drives are graded, a forecourt made, changes in level exploited, and perhaps a dam or artificial lake put in.

The drive should be the first part of the garden to be designed. Both the journey and the arrival can be exciting experiences in a country garden if the drive is designed properly. A sense of expectancy and pleasure builds if it takes its time, perhaps winding in a big loop around the property, offering intriguing glimpses of landscape features – a lake or dam, a stand of trees, a sculpture in a secluded spot – and rooftops through the trees.

The driveway is a border, a transitional state, not the heart of the garden. I love driveways that end at a forecourt to the house. In the past the forecourt was born of practical necessity – it needed to be big enough for horses and carriages and lots of service vehicles to pull up on – but its scale remains aesthetically right. A long driveway that suddenly opens out to become an expanse of gravel before a gracious house sets the whole mood of a visit or a return.

A country garden has the space to change subtly as it moves away from the house; to become less formal. It might start with garden rooms close to the house, but these might eventually lead into avenues or paths that cross woodland or grass. A country garden can also evolve; it needs a master plan for the core elements and articulation of the main axes at the start, but there is space for new parts to develop over time. They are not static places, country gardens.

Often country holdings have heart-stopping views and the temptation is to open the garden out to embrace the whole. But by restricting the views a little, by framing them with hedges or groups of trees, they become a focus rather than a backdrop. The visitor wants to move around the garden, to discover all its surprises and sudden vistas, instead of gazing on it from one fixed, passive point such as a doorway or the terrace.

To me designing for the country is not about clashes or contrasts. I don't like hard surfaces in the country; in a funny way softer gardens than those of the city work best. If the environment is harsh, they become an oasis; if temperate, they blend with their landscape. Specifically I like gravel for driveways (there are few other options for a long drive, in any case) and always try to source a local gravel, then the colour does not jump out but is part of the natural spectrum. The gravel should be continued into the forecourt so that there is no abrupt break, and hard paving restricted to high-traffic areas. Elsewhere – paths, terraces, steps and banks – soft surfaces can translate into lawn. Even around swimming pools lawn can run right to the water's edge.

To drive through dry bush and find at the end the tranquillity of a lawn is one of the ultimate experiences. More and more in designing for the country I am reshaping and sculpting earth, then covering it with lawn or grass. Exciting work. Of course in Australia designers and gardeners have to be careful about how much lawn they employ unless they have a high rainfall or a private dam, although picking a drought-tolerant type helps.

Long grass is a fashion, but a practical one because it can be left to dry out in summer. A large field of grass comes alive with the wind. Sculpting grass – varying the heights, introducing the contrast of short-mown parts and high, unmown ones – interests me for future projects. The tall grass usually needs to be mechanically slashed every two months and a path through it mown every second week. 'Textured grass', lawn mown into patterns, is rather fascinating, but a little too precious for the Australian country.

Just as surfaces should be kept soft in colour and texture so the dominant planting in a country garden should harmonise with the broader setting. This can mean using Australian trees and shrubs native to the particular area or a similar one – the blackwood *Acacia melanoxylon*, for example, is appropriate to many gardens. But it can also mean buying in local nurseries and planting extensively the types of introduced trees associated with the history of settlement in that area. They are not indigenous to it, but their form and colouring are in harmony with it. It's like that at the beach: salt-resistant plants look right, whatever their origins.

Many Australian country gardens abut bushland. The French have traditionally dealt well with such an interface. They shut out but do not totally conceal the trees beyond by setting a strict hedge between garden and wood. Alternatively, trees grown in front of the hedge will blur the boundary between garden and native forest, while a ha-ha (perhaps framed by hedges on either side) will separate the two areas but leave open a view to the trees. The formality of hedges or ha-has juxtaposed with the looseness of bush intensifies not only the sense of the garden as a haven, but also an awareness of the difference between the made (the 'civilised') and the natural.

Traditionally, large country gardens were quite detailed and diverse in their planting, but the trend needs to be away from that. I think en masse planting is even more important for the unity of the garden in the country than it is in town. Five metres of irises, five of daisies and five of lavender in a deep bed – or separate beds – has much greater impact than interspersed species. Simpler is more spectacular – and it's also easier to maintain.

Time, like space, is on a different scale in the country. Patience is needed. In the city people often want a finished garden straight away: neighbouring buildings need to be blocked out or the property needs to be resold after a couple of years. In the country trees take ten to fifteen years to mature (much more if they are oaks), and designs take time to evolve and be executed.

As long as the segments designed are large it doesn't matter if they are designed at different times. As long as the same philosophy applies the whole will seem integrated. Strong axes and vistas, the overscaling of proportions and features, simplicity of planting, the predominance of greens and textures – the principles of balance don't change. They provide a constant that pulls the parts together. The garden can afford to take its time. Besides, an instant garden is like Christmas: all the presents at once and then it's over.

olive trees, planted to create a cross-axis that leads visitors further into the first rose garden, will mature into an avenue on a scale with the garden (opposite page).

Mature trees in the land beyond the house's walled garden – and through which the drive winds – allow the distinctive Palladian villa to sit comfortably in its Australian country setting (previous pages).

SOMETIMES designing a country garden means starting with a breathtaking site – and, in this instance, an unusual house. The house stands on a cliff top, with an uninterrupted view of the ocean. The owners and the interior designer John Coote had travelled to the Veneto in Italy to study the sixteenth-century architecture of Andrea Palladio, and returned to build a Palladian villa.

The property was once a dairy farm of 20 or so hectares, and some fine, old cypresses and oak trees remained: utilising these, John Coote and I designed a drive that wound around parkland, offering glimpses of house and ocean, before straightening to become a long, formal approach to a gravel forecourt in front of the villa. The house design is perfectly symmetrical and so the garden layout became equally symmetrical, and strung out along the axis of the driveway with the villa itself as the main focus (or the ocean, looking down the axis from the house). Privet (*Ligustrum vulgare*) hedges to 400 millimetres high planted on either side of the drive reinforced the central axis. The cliff is whipped by fierce, salty winds so a higher than usual (2.4-metre) wall had to be built around the entire garden in order for the plants the owners wanted to flourish; even the entry to the garden is closed by a wooden gate when the winds blow.

The ground plan that evolved consisted of a first section with four garden beds of equal size, two on either side of the driveway; a middle circle of cypress hedging split by the axis; and a third garden, also divided by the drive, closest to the house. To either side of the front of the house lie additional walled gardens: a swimming-pool courtyard and a picking garden. The design, although echoing the symmetry and formalism of the villa, is not based on a sixteenth-century Italian garden. The owners wanted the foundation planting to be roses and the layout was devised to meet that wish.

The showcase became the four square beds, outlined in English box (*Buxus sempervirens*) and set in lawn, with the remaining two sections of the garden quieter, more reflective areas. Each bed was given as its centrepiece an iron obelisk, designed by me, to take climbing roses; and each bed a different colour scheme: one holds yellow and white roses; another red roses; a third creams; and the last apricots and pinks. The roses are underplanted with traditional perennials – irises, sedums, euphorbias and *Alchemilla mollis*. The garden walls in this part are lined with 3-metre-high *Magnolia grandiflora* 'Little Gem'.

The circular middle room of the garden was created solely by the hedges of Leyland cypress (x *Cupressocyparis leylandii*) to wall height, with a planting of rosemary at their base. In the final room, nearest the house, vigorous Rugosa roses were planted against the garden walls. In the centre of both parts of the Rugosa garden were built long but very shallow ornamental pools, the interiors coated black so that they reflect the clouds moving across the wide country sky. Between the pools and the roses there is only grass – the whole is simple but strong in keeping with the old roses.

Because of the scale and style of the walled garden and its house, it was appropriate to add complexity to the ground plan by establishing secondary cross-axes. The first was formed by an avenue of olive trees (*Olea europaea*) planted to bisect the ornamental rose garden. Stepping stones set between the avenue of olives on both sides lead to an urn elevated to just below wall height. The pale green of the olive trees contrasts well with the dark green of the magnolias, and the cypresses further on; and of course olive trees, like cypresses, add an echo of Italy in the garden. A second cross-axis was created by the placement of two substantial wall fountains, built on site, on either side of the circular room. The reflective pools fulfil the same function in the Rugosa garden.

The walled vegetable garden is as formal as the main garden. It was designed for easy access and to look good all year despite its seasonal nature. A series of metal arches was run the length of one side, over a path giving access to four parallel vegetable beds separated by four more gravel paths. In time fruiting pear trees espaliered on the arches will form a splendid tunnel. Four iron seats set in the four aisles allow people to enjoy the vegetable beds. Each bed is edged with hedges of box and divided into four triangular compartments by clipped lines of the lavender *Lavandula angustifolia*, which meet in the centre at an iron obelisk that takes climbing vegetables such as beans and zucchini. It's a highly productive garden, the vegetables regularly rotated in the compartments. The owners are grand-parents, and they like giving their grandchildren areas in which to grow vegetables in a part of the garden they spend much time in themselves.

The swimming-pool courtyard is simpler: the pool is set in grass, and fruiting figs (*Ficus carica*) behind low hedges of box line the walls.

The different garden rooms opening out on either side, as you progress along the central driveway to the house, give a sense of a grand garden but in fact neither the layout nor the ornamentation chosen was elaborate: it had been far more important to ensure they were on a scale with the house – and most important of all to ensure that neither competed with the Palladian villa. The villa commands the viewer's immediate attention and will continue to do so.

IN ORDER TO GROW
the fruit, vegetables and roses the owners wanted, extra-high walls had to be built. Even then in the vegetable garden the pear trees trained on a series of arches were in danger of being hurt by the salty prevailing winds so an even higher cypress hedge had to be grown on the far side of one wall.

IN THE HEART of a peppermint-gum forest, in the heart of a small valley, I built an enclosed garden some years ago. It is part of a winery at Margaret River, an area of Western Australia famous for its vineyards, but it is trees, not rows of vines, that surround it.

The house is essentially an L-shaped complex of pavilions built on two levels. Together with a long garden wall running parallel to the driveway, and a lillypilly (*Acmena smithii*) hedge added by me on the fourth side, the pavilions enclose the garden.

Colonnades run the length of the garden on both sides; two further colonnades cross the garden. A guest pavilion forms the short side of the L; the long side of the L is formed by two pavilions housing the living rooms and the master bedroom. One of the cross-colonnades separates the guest pavilion from the main courtyard, which the living pavilion faces; the second separates the main courtyard from a lower one into which the master bedroom looks.

Visitors alight on the driveway, enter through a tall portico, follow a colonnade across the garden and arrive at the front door in the centre of the main pavilion. Although the complex's outer windows face the creek and bush, the pavilions and their courtyards are essentially inward-looking.

The buildings were half-constructed and the garden space defined by the time I was called in so the work of the design was to further link the pavilions and to make sense of the levels. The space was ample to work with and the change of level introduced the interest of developing two courtyards.

My first task, however, was to ensure the long driveway provided a proper transition and not a blunt division between natural bush and formal courtyards. To achieve this I planted an avenue that consisted of the pear tree *Pyrus nivalis*, which have olive-green foliage almost the colour of the eucalypts' leaves. The drive itself was made with local gravel, which like the avenue of trees blends with the natural setting. I continued the pear trees in a line along the wall separating the garden from the driveway so that their tops form an upper storey for the plants inside the courtyards.

The garden the owner and I planned could be high-maintenance because she is absorbed in the whole process of gardening. Her primary request was for a series of rose gardens underplanted with irises; she is mad about both. She selected the roses and irises, and I worked out how best to display them. Since Margaret River is slightly cooler than Perth, we were able to grow complementary plants, such as English box and crab-apple trees, which find Perth too hot.

The owner's second request was that I incorporate into the design two huge, ribbed terracotta oil jars she already possessed. It was quite stimulating to start with the ornamentation; normally designers work in the reverse order. For the centre of the main courtyard I designed a long waterlily pond – built a little higher than its outline of box hedging so that the pool appears to float – then set the oil jars on semicircular ledges at either end (see pages 126–7). The aligned jars reinforce the main axis that runs through the courtyards. Simple ornamentation, used simply. There is not even a fountain – moving water would have been in competition with the jars.

The only other ornaments in the main courtyard are four tall, overscaled (3.5-metre) metal obelisks topped with a ball, rather like those in the previous garden discussed, which we placed in the corners. The owner wanted climbing roses and we could keep them safe from the possums if we grew them on obelisks because possums don't like operating at ground level. The scale of the obelisks and oil jars dictated the size of the stepping-stone pavers I wanted to set in local gravel for the

THE YOUNG CRAB-APPLE
walk leads from one of the two colonnades crossing the garden to a large oil jar placed against a lillypilly hedge at the end of the garden. Beyond is a forest of peppermint gums (opposite page).

The two jars that are the only addition to the long lily pond in the main courtyard are uplit at night, but much of the garden itself is left rather shadowy and mysterious (following pages).

horizontal surface: about 1.2 metres by 1.2 metres. Since nothing was commercially available in this size, they were poured in situ and matched in tone to the sandstone pillars.

The dimensions of the main courtyard – about 12 metres by 20 metres – allowed us to have 2-metre-deep flowerbeds, excellent for roses. We adorned the enclosing colonnades with wisteria. Against the garden wall we built an arbour, now covered in climbing roses and star jasmine (*Trachelospermum jasminoides*), so that people could sit and enjoy the garden (see pages 130–1). The vineyard's soil is rich and the rainfall good: everything thrives here. The quite intense reds and pinks of the roses chosen give the whole planting an almost tropical look that enhances the deeply romantic effect of the colonnades.

The lower courtyard I decided to turn into a walk, once again using outsized pavers as stepping stones set in gravel, with trees planted in lawn on either side (see page 125). I chose crab apples because it's quite a small walk – only five trees long. A lovely crab-apple walk can be easily kept at a height of 3 or 4 metres for its entire life. Adjacent to the lawn and in front of the wall separating the garden from the driveway, a deep flowerbed was given a 'castellated' outline: Rugosa roses fill its bays. The crab apple *Malus spectabilis*, with its strong pink blossoms, was selected to complement the Rugosas.

The trees bloom at the same time as the roses and, like the roses, stay in flower for a long time. We purchased a third oil jar to link the two parts of the garden and set it against the lillypilly hedge at the end of the walk, completing the elaboration of the main axis. At the far end also, to either side of the walk, are two series of metal arches that form rose-draped tunnels, one leading to steps ascending to the drive, the other to the creek. Each is about 3 metres wide and 3 metres high.

The two courtyards combined suggest quite elaborate detail in a very formal area, but not unnecessary detail. The scale of this country garden and the length of its main axis allow a complexity – for example, of flowerbed shapes and colonades – not possible in most urban gardens. Yet for all its refinement it has a country feel: partly it is the scale, but partly also the backdrop of valley and natural forest. And while the house is not in the Australian vernacular (although a wide verandah does overlook the creek), the colonnades create the sense of a rural house open to the garden.

At night the oil jars, some of the columns and the edges of the crab-apple walk are uplit, and of course all the steps are lit for safety. But I don't believe you should go overboard with lighting in a country garden. It doesn't need to be lit up like a Christmas tree. Rather, lighting should heighten our awareness of night in the country – of deep darkness pricked by pinpoints of light.

OVERSIZED PAVERS,
like the rectangular lily pond and its oil jars, emphasise the long axis that carries the eye through the two courtyards (opposite page).

Lushness is assured by the wisteria draping the colonnades, the star jasmine and roses twining around the pillars of the arbour, the climbing roses on their metal obelisks and the deep beds filled with roses and irises (following pages).

ONE OF THE TWO

matching fountains built for the country courtyard to introduce some solidity and symmetry (opposite page).

Anduze pots, placed to reinforce the symmetry introduced into the otherwise asymmetrical courtyard by the two fountains, add weight to the courtyard corners without competing with the fountains (following pages).

THIS WALLED courtyard is one part of an extensive country garden I have designed that has many parts to it, including a polo field. What I had to work with was an L-shaped area, with both sides of the L about 10 metres by 25 metres: not a symmetrical shape but nevertheless a blank canvas, apart from its existing sandstone walls.

It isn't a courtyard with any of the problems of tiny walled courtyards, described in the next section of this book: it's large, well watered by rains, sun-filled and ventilated. In fact it has too much ventilation — forceful winds soon made me decide the openwork gate wouldn't do. It's not a courtyard into which major rooms look; rather it's one to which the family retreats on days when the winds makes the other parts of the garden less habitable. It has been quite traditional in European architecture to have a private courtyard even when the grounds are extensive, and that is how I saw this courtyard. It is entered from the house by a door at the end of a minor passageway; the courtyard opens up to the viewer only once they have stepped into it, and even then only the first side of the L is visible. Consequently what I did was make the width of this first part, rather than the line from passageway to facing wall, the main axis. By placing a matching fountain at either end of this main axis, a qualified symmetry was introduced: qualified because in the second part of the L only one of the fountains can be seen and then side on. Squares of paving — consisting of four pavers each — set in gravel further connect the two fountains.

The starting point for the fountains' design was a fine old stone carving of a head that I had had for some time, waiting for the right time to use it. The head seemed perfect for the Mediterranean atmosphere of the courtyard, and a stonemason was on hand to carve a replica for the second fountain. With such a skilled craftsman it was also possible to have two distinctive sandstone fountain-backs carved. The shape doesn't conform strictly to any one style: it's just one I thought would be chunky enough for the courtyard — and one that would be thrown into interesting relief by the sun. Porous Western Australian sandstone ages quickly: already moss on the deep troughs makes the fountains look as if they have stood in their place for years. At the corners of the courtyard I created recesses in the wide, raised beds that I had run along the garden walls to hold Anduze pots planted with citrus trees — apart from the fountains the only other, equally elemental, ornamentation. The walls of the courtyard were clothed in either wisteria, on wires, or *Magnolia grandiflora* 'Little Gem' grown in the beds, behind English box hedging. The property has a newly completed, extensive vegetable garden, but the courtyard allows herbs and flowers planted in the beds to be quickly picked for the house.

It has been quite traditional in European architecture to have a private courtyard even when the grounds are extensive, and that is how I saw this courtyard.

ST AMBROSE FARM, my own place, is, like the property just discussed, a garden in progress. Parts of it are established; parts of it are in the development stage; and parts of it are just a glimmer of a plan at the back of my mind.

The property at Woodend – an easy drive from my city office – is a bit over 1 hectare and roughly triangular. The house appears to be at the far end of the land, but in fact the 'apex' of the triangle lies, unused, beyond a fence to the west.

The house had an instant powerful appeal when I first saw it several years ago. It was quite quirky: not a traditional house at all but, rather, an old derelict rural school. Its playing fields had turned to weed and except for several trees – notably a few huge cypresses in one corner – there was no sign of planting. I could do something unusual with this, I thought, surveying the deserted house and empty grounds. It was obvious that the school was well positioned on the block. It sat right against the long, southern boundary, yet appeared to nestle into the gum trees of the State forest behind it. This left a good expanse of land in front of the school, to the north.

It was three or four months before I had a feeling for the form the school conversion and new garden should take, although it was obvious, given the block's size, that the work would have to be undertaken in several stages, starting with the house section. Once I did, I got the structure of the garden – the lines, levels and layout – pretty right first off because I knew that dividing the land into rooms (large rooms to match the scale of the schoolrooms and the block) would allow

WISTERIA ALONG THE

verandah, pots of topiary and an edging of Lonicera nitida *and slightly higher English box along the façade of St Ambrose Farm both bring the house into the garden and soften the view across the overscaled forecourt and fountain in daylight or night light.*

different parts to fulfil different functions without the whole seeming disparate, would give logic to the garden's unfolding.

To exploit the land facing the house to the full, the drive needed to hug the northern boundary. To heighten a sense of expectancy, visitors would be given only glimpses of the house's high roofline, and the tops of two garden statues, through a narrow avenue of pear trees (*Pyrus calleryana* 'Bradford') contained within the walls of a high privet (*Ligustrum vulgare*) hedge. At the end of the drive they would curve round to pass through double gates, near the north-western corner, and into a forecourt.

The forecourt I decided to treat in the grand European manner. I wanted to match the scale of the garden to that of the large classrooms, with their 5.5-metre-high ceilings. As a consequence the forecourt is as enormous as that of a manor house, but the overscaling works because the rooms of the small school are intrinsically overscaled. Paradoxically the huge but uncluttered forecourt settles the modest schoolhouse in the landscape. The driveway was surfaced with oversized local pebbles, which were continued into the forecourt, their size reinforcing the robust character of the court. There were practical as well as aesthetic reasons for my choosing to have such a large forecourt: it needed to provide plenty of parking for cars on its western side and sufficient space in front of the house for tables to be carried outside for parties.

At the centre of the forecourt I set an enormous ornamental pool: it's a very traditional thing to do, and essential in rural Australia, I think, to counteract the summer heat. It was constructed from rendered brick and unadorned except for four balls of box grown at each corner. From its centre leaps a forceful line of water. Any further ornamentation would have made the forecourt seem pretentious so I merely softened the effect of the pebbled expanse and heavy pool with deep flowerbeds, lined with *Tilia cordata* 'Greenspire' trees around the perimeters, and made the conjunction of forecourt and house less abrasive by the addition of low double hedges of lonicera and box, vines of lilac-blue wisteria, and clipped box in large concrete pots.

The forecourt is essentially the first of the several garden rooms. Enclosed on three sides by privet hedges itself, it leads to rooms hedged in privet to its north and east. The proportions of each room had to be established at the outset so that the construction of levels could start. The budget can quickly get out of control on a country property. I economised throughout by using just sleepers for retaining walls, hidden by the hedges planted in front of them, or batters (slopes) of grass. The construction of the levels was mainly a cut-and-fill job done by two big bulldozers, with some topsoil brought in to compensate for the clay.

When the forecourt first went in, I did worry that this time I really had exceeded the bounds of overscaling: despite the importance of the north–south axis, someone seated inside or outside the sitting room could not look into the garden room to the north because of the size of the forecourt. Now, however, with all the plants flourishing that has already become irrelevant: the leafy tilias offer sufficient pleasure in themselves and tie the forecourt to the leafiness of the other parts of the garden.

I designed three wide steps to lead down to the northern garden. The room was strung along the major north–south axis, which I defined with a broad path of lawn that carries the eye to a distant statue set in a recess of hedge. A second broad path of lawn bisects the first and is marked at either end by inconspicuous wooden benches.

This was to be my vegetable garden: four square beds, divided into triangular compartments by lines of box hedging – a traditional layout that had allowed gardeners to rotate their crops. Frames of espaliered Jonathan apples were placed against the backdrop of the tall hedge walls (see pages 140–1). At their feet I planted strawberries. Pebble paths around each bed were intended to make picking the fruit and vegetables easy. Each bed was decorated at its corners with a cone of box, and the compartments of each bed met at an elevated, central Anduze urn holding a clipped ball of box.

The room exists for uncomplicated pleasure: as a wide, sunny garden of soft effects and vivacious contrasts that invites visitors who venture there from the forecourt to linger and unwind. The east room, adjacent to both the forecourt and the north room, is more intense (see pages 2–3 and 114–15). The intensity depends on the elongation of the room – actual and illusory – and the strongly controlled movement that that creates. The room is divided in two (and also intersected by the major, east–west axis discussed below): walls of hedge part just enough to reveal its northern half. Six 'stepping stones' of water, set directly in the lawn of the southern half, lead the eye through this opening to a very dark, very narrow 20-metre-long ornamental pool. It too is set level with the lawn, and it too directs the eye beyond, to a statue raised against a background of green. A series of hedged bays enclosing crab-apple trees, not competing statues, became the only other ornamentation in this second half of the room; four E-shaped hedges of box, placed on either side of the line of stepping-stone pools, became the only additional decoration in the first. The overscaling, the hyper-greenness, the iconic E-shapes, the strong sense of enclosure, make this part of the garden an introverted, contemplative experience.

Detailed planting ideas for the forecourt and northern room were developed only once the structure of the garden was clear, and in a somewhat evolutionary way. Initially I tended to go down that country road of lots of plants and flowers. Cold winters, with frosts and occasional snow, mild summers and a high rainfall provide the Woodend area with an ideal climate for growing many of the perennials and other plants that normally do not flourish in Australia. The area's rich gardening heritage and interesting nurseries had been part of St Ambrose Farm's attraction for me, and it seemed natural to acknowledge its gardening traditions in my own design.

In the forecourt I've arrived by a process of elimination at the perennials *Petasites fragrans* and *Alchemilla mollis*. The petasites thrust forward big, kidney-shaped leaves on 1-metre-high stalks so that the tilias seem to be buoyed by air cushions. Corymbs of greenish cream flowerheads, which appear in late winter before the leaves, are simply a bonus. The many-lobed, light green leaves of the alchemilla edging the beds, and their froth of tiny green flowers over a number of months, make them a superior perennial. Along either side of the path leading to the fenced-off, unused land on the west, deep rows of *Sedum* 'Autumn Joy' complete the greens – except when their pale green flowerheads turn pinkish bronze in autumn.

When I came to plant the ornamental vegetable beds in the northern room a dreadful realisation occurred: even if I picked only one lettuce it would leave a gap, and I couldn't bear the beds to look patchy during the warm months! So I turned again to perennials. Not the green-flowered perennials of the forecourt, however, because the northern room needed to have its own character. For the moment I have settled on the soft blue catmint *Nepeta* x *faassenii* and the red-veined ornamental dock *Rumex sanguineus*, planted in alternate triangles of the beds.

Big gardens suggest a multiplicity of effects, but that isn't the case at St Ambrose. Simplicity has been the guiding principle. Hedging, lawn and creamy pebbles are used again and again, their repetition tying the different parts of the garden together. Ornamentation is restricted to a few objects, used purposefully, and natural elements such as water and plants – the water features themselves being pared back to their essential form, and the range and arrangement of plants simplified.

Stage two of the garden at St Ambrose is slowly progressing. The intrinsic movement in this garden is, despite the important north–south sight-lines, east–west since the property is much longer than it is wide. That axis runs through the middle of the forecourt and its fountain. On the eastern (road) side, as I mentioned in the book's Introduction, I've defined the east–west axis beyond the east room with a sunken, grassy walkway beneath an avenue of *Tilia cordata* 'Greenspire' that leads to an overscaled, elevated urn – the first task before the design for the land on that side can be fully developed. My philosophy hasn't changed, the main axes won't change, so the garden can develop at its own pace.

ONE OF THE FOUR

ornamental beds in the north room off the forecourt, with the blossom of espaliered Jonathan apples in the background (following pages).

The longest, east–west axis of the garden (much foreshortened in the photograph) bisects the forecourt and the first section of the east room, and is punctuated by the fountain and a new avenue of tilias beyond the east room. It culminates in a high urn elevated near the street boundary against a 'borrowed' background of mature trees (pages 142–3).

OVERLOOKING THE SEA, two joined properties are home to three generations of one family. A few years ago I was asked to build a garden that would suit the extended family, the beach setting and the renovations an architect was engaged in drawing up. The two original houses were fairly nondescript so the architect was able to add a striking gateway between them and equally striking pergolas, facing the sea, for both. One of the properties has a tennis court at the front, for which the architect designed a pavilion in the form of an elevated formal pergola (the land rises between the two blocks) and a grand staircase curving up to it on either side (see pages 146–7).

The owners wanted a garden with a feel of the south of France about it. I began at the beginning, with the driveway, added on one side of the front garden. In went an avenue of the pear tree *Pyrus calleryana* 'Bradford', with clumps of the lavender *Lavandula angustifolia*, *Santolina chamaecyparissus* and irises , for the whole 150-metre length of the drive. Already the two lines of pear trees are reaching out to each other across the 3 metres that separate them. Salt winds do burn pear trees, but these ones are protected by the house lying between them and the sea.

Halfway along the drive we made an entry that provides access to the tennis pavilion and court. For the area between I designed a lawn with a grove of olive trees — these are trees that certainly won't be burnt by salt winds. At the base of the pavilion's retaining wall, between the wings of the double stairway, I placed a wall fountain that continued the Mediterranean overtones introduced by the plantings. With its massive arch, it is reminiscent of an ancient Roman aqueduct.

INTERCEPTING AND EDGING
bands of light-coloured cement prevent the main, darker cement of the long front drive on the double block from becoming monotonous. The land sloped too much for gravel to be an option – it would have washed away.

MEDITERRANEAN-INSPIRED plantings, which include olive trees, pencil pines, irises and espaliered magnolias in addition to the cycads seen in the photograph, have sufficient strength and vitality to balance the stairway in the 'courtyard' between the two houses on the property (above).

A classical god's head, mounted on the keystone of the fountain-back, dribbles water into a break-front pool. The scale of the fountain is in keeping with that of the elevated tennis-court pergola – and the large front garden shared by the two houses.

Encroaching greenery, in the form of espaliered lemon trees planted on either side, heighten the effect. Above, wisteria over time will drape the carved wooden pergola beams I added to the architect's pillars. Pergola, stairs and fountain combined make a powerful decorative statement – permissible because the front garden is so extensive and the façades of the houses so low-key.

Between the two parallel houses the architect inserted what was essentially a partially walled court-yard to give both a little separation (see previous page). I worked with him on the design of a flight of steps up to the gateway leading to the garden at the front of the higher house. The stairs were interrupted halfway up by a landing, accentuated with a pergola, the pillars of which received carved wooden beams matching those of the tennis pavilion. On the landing a cushion of English box on either side appears to support an Anduze pot of the cycad *Cycas revoluta*, enhancing the considerable presence of the stairway.

Unlike the front garden, which has its distinct areas of tennis court, lawns and driveway, the back garden is all open space facing the sea. Here I added just four double-sided 12-metre to 15-metre long beds, with strips of grass between. Down the centre of each bed I ran lavender, with trimmed balls of santolina to either side. The santolina loves the sun, loves the sand, loves the salt. And so too does the lavender. Combined, they offer a perfect example of the way massed plantings work in big gardens beyond cities even more than they do in smaller gardens within cities.

BANDS OF SANTOLINA
and lavender look spectacular but don't impede the view of the sea from the back garden. 'Borrowed' gum trees and tea trees give the area all the height and background it requires.

The santolina and lavender (and a cypress hedge) provide a flourishing garden in a coastal environment where that's hard to achieve (following pages).

COURTYARD

Tiny courtyards, light wells, rooftop gardens and balconies: balance in these difficult environments can only be relative. These are essentially rooms that lead on from house or apartment rooms so that's how they must be treated: as extra rooms, needing all the attention to detail and design that an interior does, particularly since they will probably be used or viewed as much at night as during the day.

Like rooms, these gardens can be taken in at a glance. There's no point in trying to pretend they are something they are not, no possibility of totally hiding where they stop or start. So essentially the garden maker has to be bold and play up the boundary: erect a trellis on it; place a feature in front of it; add panelling to it and grow creepers in the recesses. It's working with what's there rather than trying to work against it.

Just two palms against a blue sky, on a rooftop of marble and water, create the mirage of a garden (page 153). This rooftop 'garden' is featured on pages 166–7.

A traditional herb garden seemed the obvious choice for a kitchen courtyard continually on view, but with no through traffic (pages 154–5). It was neither large enough nor sunny enough for any herb except parsley, but the contrast of bright green parsley with darker, neater English box hedging makes the courtyard a rejuvenating experience: tranquil and invigorating at the same time.

A slight blurring of the boundaries is possible in a tiny courtyard if a full-length mirror can be added. The mirror needs to be pitted and aged – genuinely or deliberately – and slightly tilted so that it only dimly reflects greenery rather than catches everything in the garden, particularly people. A creeper spilling around the edges will further help the deception.

Rooftop and balcony gardens often have high-rise buildings next to them, but a balance of scale is rarely achievable: usually you can't put trees up there. What you can do is grow creepers to eye level so that there's at least an illusion of balance – and some sort of contact with nature immediately beyond the doors and windows of the interior. And the vertical plane can be exploited to the maximum. Lines of wisteria can frame a space, suggesting a tree when there is none.

Where a view of the city skyline or the tops of trees gives a garden breadth and should not be impeded, as in the case of some rooftops or balconies, ornamentation may need to be two matched urns, say, placed against the side boundaries, rather than one urn positioned against the most prominent boundary. Traditionally an urn has been set quite high on a plinth or on house or garden architecture – at eye level, viewed from the opposite end of the sight-line. In an intimate space an object or objects placed centrally but almost at the viewer's feet is an alternative, as the rooftop garden that ends this book shows.

Just like the room it essentially is, a tiny courtyard or a rooftop garden needs good lighting. This is one of those rare times when more is better: the more you light its main components, the more interesting it is going to look from inside and the more you are going to want to step out and use it at night. Illuminate all features, as much of the plant material as you can, and the whole space sufficiently to be able to move easily around it.

Treating these areas as a pocket dining or sitting room is irresistible when size allows. It is even possible to cook in them, although a barbecue in a small space does pose a problem. One that can be hidden in a slide-out drawer when not in use is perhaps the best solution. Similarly heating or air-conditioning units, bins, hot-water services or other utilitarian items that have to occupy the space are difficult to disguise, but can be tidied up by being enclosed. It's essential not to have a lot of disparate shapes and objects on show.

Although the opposite should be true, heavy furniture often works well. It gives a small area substance and can't blow away or flap around dangerously. However, using a limited outdoor space as an added room doesn't mean that something as practical as a dining table or a sun lounge should ever be the focal point, or be allowed to obscure the focal point.

As always, the cue for the style and materials should come from the building – and, in these kinds of gardens, from the adjacent rooms also. The colour of the interior walls can be picked up outside, and the fabrics on sofas repeated on soft upholstery to be taken outside. Doing this can give a neutral area a strength it doesn't have intrinsically. Inevitably a hard material such as paving will have to cover most of the horizontal surface of a light well or rooftop garden. Repeating or complementing the interior flooring is always the most appropriate response when that's feasible.

As for plants in the types of gardens considered here, there's no escaping the unpalatable fact that they're hard to introduce and they're hard to maintain. For a start most of these gardens experience light and shade difficulties. If they get full sunlight, their hard surfaces soon turn them into heat traps: there is nowhere for the warmth to go so it continues to build up. The reverse happens if they are continually in shade. And sometimes these gardens can both receive too much sunlight on one side and not enough on the other. To plant the two sides differently would look odd in a small area so the few plants that do well in both situations – *Lonicera nitida*, box, lillypilly, ivy, Boston ivy – are the only options. Choice is taken away from you. All you can do is simplify.

The same is true where lack of ventilation makes airborne pests and diseases a major problem. Succulents don't do so well because they like more light than fully enclosed small courtyards and light wells usually receive, but a limited range of plants such as ivy, Boston ivy, box and certain types of lilies thrive.

With apartment 'gardens' – rooftops, balconies, spots on top of car-park lids – there's not even any soil, or the possibility of adding much because the loading (weight per square metre) would be a problem. Light planter boxes are one way around this. Fibreglass liners made to size can be inserted in a cement-sheeting case, which is then acrylic-rendered to match the building. Or wooden planter boxes can be constructed if wood is an important material of the building. I tend not to buy standard ready-made troughs because they can look like an afterthought to the design.

Rooftop areas at least are by no means always small, but the limitations remain; they usually can't be turned into densely planted, tree-filled gardens. The only possibility is to create generous dining and sun-baking terraces, softened with plants in pots and planters and shaded by canvas awnings or umbrellas (or a light pergola if regulations allow). Water too is heavy so rooftop water features need to be shallow.

Wind is always a huge problem on rooftops and balconies. The only solutions are to keep plants below the balustrade line; to select hardy varieties such as cacti, succulents and box, and ones that don't have flowers that the wind can batter and bruise; and to rely on architectural features rather than plants for effect.

Exposed gardens dry out fast so good irrigation is essential. A dripper system works well, provided there is a tap available. Drainage is a problem when there is no ground to carry water away naturally – and sometimes a nightmare when someone else's ceiling is just below.

These kinds of gardens must drain well and to one point where there is a downpipe in place.

Despite the appropriateness, in theory, of having plants in pots as the major focus in tiny gardens, often an architectural feature, such as an urn, an obelisk or a light fountain, is the better adornment to avoid relying on living matter that needs constant care to survive. I always feel sad when, a few years after a rooftop or light-well garden has been established, the clients ring in bewilderment to say that all their plants are scruffy, struggling or even dead. The truth is that's often the fate of plants in these gardens. In Europe and New York apartments people throw their plants out every year and replace them.

The one advantage with essentially short-life, dispensable gardens is that you can follow fashion more closely. Regarding whether or not a garden should be influenced by fashion, there's a strange sort of sliding scale according to size. With a large country property you are creating for the future, there's a permanency about whatever you build that has to be kept in mind. With an urban block you are often establishing a family garden that might span a generation, but after that pass into other hands, be subdivided, deteriorate. With a tiny space you are designing a garden that might last only two or three years so you can be as avant-garde as you wish. In the most extreme case, where there is absolutely no natural light, just pebbles and a jet of water might be all that's added. I have designed tiny gardens like that and enjoyed the look of them. Are they still gardens? I think so. Certainly they are balanced.

WHAT TO DO with a tiny, 2-metre by 5-metre garden between the cast-iron fence and the verandah of a Victorian terrace house? It offered no space at all really and was certainly not a garden that people could use. Yet as the introduction to the house it needed to offer a promise of lovely things to come. I decided on a garden that could best be viewed from the path leading to the front door. A hedge of lillypilly (*Acmena smithii*) on three sides to a height of 1.2 metres (the height of the fence) achieved that without creating an oppressive enclosure. It became a very geometric, very patterned courtyard, the ground paved in a chequerboard of pebbles and baby's tears (*Soleirolia soleirolii*). At the far end was set a low bowl with a single jet of water (the water drains into a hidden sump with a pump and is reticulated). More pebbles were placed within the bowl. The baby's tears grow evenly in their diamonds because the area is uniformly shady and they are never crushed underfoot.

The property has a further courtyard at the back, trapped between the house and a converted stable, with windows onto the area. Here I was able to carry the Indian sandstone pavers of the kitchen into the garden, giving them an edging and a central circular motif consisting of pebbles (the same pebbles as in the front courtyard) set in cement. On the side boundaries, to provide privacy and utilise the vertical plane, I designed a 'three-dimensional' iron frame (as distinct from wires on the walls) on which to support pleached 'trees' of wisteria. In time the wisteria 'trees' will offer a solid canopy in summer, with sufficient decorative 'branches' in winter to provide a visual barrier when the wisteria is bare. Below the wisteria, tiers of English box (*Buxus sempervirens*) and *Trachelospermum asiaticum* were planted.

Two heavy fountains that we constructed completed the earthy feel of the courtyard. These, softened by the wisteria, face each other across the courtyard, no more than 2.5 metres apart. Around the curved moulding of one fountain-back I had 'Hydra' carved, around the other 'Aqua': Greek and Latin words with watery connotations. On the backs themselves I matched an iron spout with a line of iron balls that followed the shadow line of the moulding.

The owners, who divide their time between town and country, wanted a low-maintenance garden: the strong, simple concepts of the two small courtyards and the restricted, hardy planting schemes delivered that.

THIS INTERNAL courtyard, like the front courtyard of the previous garden, is for viewing only, even though it is much larger. Its building, a two-storey block of apartments, wraps around it on three sides. The fourth side is a high wall constructed to obscure a neighbouring building. Glass doors from the lobby of the apartment block give onto the courtyard so it is the first view that residents and visitors have as they enter the building, and is looked into by all the surrounding apartments. With a clear central axis, the courtyard offered an opportunity to design a symmetrical ground plan in keeping with the building itself. However, physical conditions in the courtyard were difficult. It is in shade for most of the day, but at certain times of the year may get two hours' full sunlight. As well, any depth of soil or ornamental water was out of the question because the courtyard is situated over the apartment block's car park. The courtyard would have to depend on a highly architectural design.

To get around the loading problem, I designed a long, rectangular, ornamental pool but made it only to a depth of about 150 millimetres. To achieve some planting space the pool was set between two beds 200 millimetres deep. This placed the pool and beds two steps up from the rest of the area, allowing water to descend from the pool into a smaller, circular one with a central jet. As so often, the inspiration was the Moorish water complexes in which water runs from a large pool along a channel to finish in a bowl. The water of the courtyard pool runs down seven shallow steps – not the courtyard's two – for greater visual impact. The rectangular pool is filled with small, black pebbles over which the water is forced, to create a perpetually shifting pattern of ripples.

The end wall of the courtyard, the climax of the major axis, was given several recesses that reinforced the lines of the horizontal surface: rectangular ones above the rectangular side beds; and a central blind arch, adorned with a god's head, to repeat the curve of the circular pool. The arch was also replicated in the shape of a window at both ends of the far wall. In fact these windows are not windows at all, but mirrors, over which metal window frames have been placed, to reflect the courtyard and make it seem larger and more mysterious.

The choice of hardy *Trachelospermum asiaticum* as a robust ground cover in the beds, and wisteria to clothe the architect's strong pergolas, overcame the planting problems of the courtyard. Two *Phoenix canariensis* palms, planted on the far side of the high end wall, will in time totally block out the neighbouring building and enfold the courtyard. The plantings, combined with the ornamental water, prevent a strongly geometric design from looking too severe. The total result is a courtyard that's very structural, very masculine, almost abstract in its effect.

THE FINISHED GARDEN
hides the problems of being built over the car park and maximises the central axis running from the apartment block's front entry to the courtyard's back wall (opposite page).

HERE'S A COMMON occurrence
these days: a wing is added to an existing house, cutting
into the garden and threatening to unbalance the relationship of garden to house. There are other parts to the
garden of this substantial house, but nevertheless in the
swimming-pool courtyard garden space was considerably reduced by the addition of a wing. Moreover the
owners wished to retain the pool.

A main (sitting-room) window looked down the
length of the swimming pool so I centred the spa that
the owners wanted at the far end and beyond it placed
an Italianate wall, divided into three panels, in front of
the high existing fence. An ornamental half-urn, framed
by the arch of the central panel, became the main feature. It was cast specially for the project since it needed to
be very tall (about 2 metres), given the scale of the wall
and the distance from which it would be viewed.

We replaced the dark brick surface of the courtyard
with pale limestone pavers so that it is now a light-filled
place of aqua, buff and green. Adding the green was the
most difficult task. Only a 500-millimetre-wide area was
left for planting once the 3-metre-wide terrace needed
for comfortable poolside lounging was built. Using the
walls became crucial. Tumbling climbers – honeysuckle,
roses and star jasmine (*Trachelospermum jasminoides*) –
create a sense of luxuriant growth. Encroaching tendrils
marry the Italianate panels to the boundary wall on either
side. Tightly clipped hedges would have made the viewer
too conscious of the looming wall, and the boundary
would have looked too blunt for a sensual water setting.
Clipped plants fulfil a different function here: Hill's weeping fig trees (*Ficus microcarpa* var. *hillii*) as standards in
tubs have been positioned strategically to give the thin
line of planting definition and depth.

THE SWIMMING POOL TAKES
*up most of the courtyard, but there is something
about water that elongates a view – its movement
draws the eye onwards. At night as the water of the
spa gently ripples, sparkling lights dance across
the ornamental wall.*

THIS FRONT GARDEN is walled off from the path leading to its Victorian villa, and is markedly lower than the verandah that runs along the house's façade. Only a bedroom and a study overlook the area so the garden, enclosed on all sides by existing high walls, is to be contemplated only, not entered – a secret garden in fact.

I lined its three garden walls with tall, pleached Hill's weeping fig trees to make the garden even more secretive. The evergreen trees create a sense of space: a second layer of planting – Boston ivy (*Parthenocissus tricuspidata*), trained against the walls – is glimpsed between the trunks and suggests that more grows here than in reality does.

The main interest of the garden, however, resides in its central planting. Because of the house's elevation and its formal style, I decided to do my own take on Elizabethan knot gardens, which were designed to be viewed primarily from the upper floors of a house. In this one the pattern is woven from two types of box, English box for the outer hedges, which enclose the weeping fig trees, and *Buxus microphylla* for the inner ones. A lower planting of baby's tears borders the English box. The baby's tears are in no way traditional to knot gardens, but the position is very shady and damp, and the looser, delicately displayed leaves contrast nicely with the formality of the box.

The knot is set within a courtyard of loose pebbles. The pattern itself is no more traditional than the baby's tears – I just doodled on paper until I had a design I liked. It needed to be quite simple because of the limited area: about 8 metres by 4 metres. And a complex knot garden would require a lot of work to develop and maintain, whereas this had to be a low-maintenance garden given its difficult access. I gave all the lines in the pattern, except those of English box, a bow-like curve to add a little elasticity. The curves help elongate the pattern and make the garden seem more than it is.

THIS ENCLOSED KNOT

garden is wholly green – except for a background note of red in autumn (opposite page). The variations on green of the two types of box used in the knot contrast with the paler green of baby's tears; the deep green of the hedges with the brighter green of the Boston ivy against the courtyard's perimeters.

Only a bedroom and a study overlook the area so the garden, enclosed on all sides by existing high walls, is to be contemplated only, not entered – a secret garden in fact.

A ROOFTOP can have minimal planting and yet still suggest a garden. An old friend of mine asked his architect uncle to design a home for him on top of a converted warehouse, and asked me to work with them both to add some garden. The resulting penthouse is essentially a wonderful glass box sitting in a moat of water. The water is a perfect way to avoid having to install a balustrade that would impede the view of the city skyline — it prevents people from going over the edges of the rooftop. And it is visually stunning. The water, only 50 millimetres deep, lies at a level just below the paving line and actually flows over the edges of the rooftop into a gutter below to be reticulated. (The building had to be reinforced to take so much weight.) We added white pebbles to the moat to intensify the visual impact of the water.

There were only two places where a barrier was required. At the front, onto which the sitting and dining rooms open, the local council required a barrier to prevent the penthouse overlooking the houses below. What the barrier needed, we decided, was a visual diversion that deflected attention from it. A planter box of sculptural *Agave attenuata*, positioned at the end of a tiny (3-metre by 1-metre) bridge added to the moat, turned out to be sufficient.

One side of the penthouse, onto which further sitting-room windows look, also required a barrier to block out neighbours. To create this the architect added a marble wall at the end of a small (7-metre by 10-metre) terrace. I designed two planter boxes to be placed on either side of the wall, but slightly to the front. In these I planted *Phoenix canariensis*. Although they are big palms, the confined planter boxes have a bonsai effect: the palms' growth will be slowed for many years. During the day the endlessly moving fronds cast fascinating shadows on the dazzling white surfaces. At night, uplit, the palms appear to float in boxes across the water.

THE PENTHOUSE

architecture looks as if it would have been incomplete without two palms, but in fact they are part of a barrier required by the local council (above left).

A line of agaves in a planter box helps preserve the privacy of the houses below, without obscuring the rooftop's view of the city beyond (opposite page).

THE MOST uninspiring areas to design gardens for are the no-man's-lands running between the blank walls of two tall buildings. This no-man's-land is in actuality the only 'garden' of a ground-floor apartment. Visitors pass it, but do not go through it, on their way to the apartment's front door. It is a narrow area, measuring only about 10 metres by 3 metres.

How to disguise that it was just a blind alley? I decided it needed tall trees to distract the eye from the high buildings on either side and to refute the narrowness. In this instance it was not an issue that trees might reinforce the verticality of the side boundaries because I knew they would arch over to form a leafy tunnel. The pear tree *Pyrus calleryana* 'Bradford' was chosen because as a more upright tree than some pears we would not be forcing it to take on an unnatural shape. As well, its fibrous, non-invasive root system would make it less likely than most to damage the adjacent walls. The brick walls on either side are different coloured so the pear trees would also help to disguise the disparate surfaces.

At the entry to the alleyway I added a low wooden gate to signify that the space was a proper garden, and because a gate always presents visitors with the temptation to open it and slip into the garden glimpsed beyond. To carry the eye the length of the garden a central path was laid leading to a fountain at the far end, which spills into a plain, rendered-brick trough. Visitors hear the water and are drawn to explore further. Only a standard 1-metre width was possible for the path but breadth was less important here, where it was length being emphasised. The pull of the path was increased by adding alternating circles and squares of dark green pebbles set in a background of pale pebbles bordered by darker pavers: a pattern can suggest a path must be longer that it is. The dark green pebbles were repeated on the fountain-back and the pavers as the capping of the trough. A spout set in a stylised flower motif formed the fountain itself.

The only other planting given the tiny garden was massed *Hydrangea macrophylla* 'Blue Wave' under the pear trees on either side of the path, and balls of English box. The width of the beds was 1 metre – less than I like but the presence of trees persuades the eye that the planting space is more generous than in fact it is. 'Blue Wave' was chosen because it flowers recurrently, but I also love the simplicity of its flat, blue-mauve lacecaps. I don't even mind it when hydrangeas are just sticks in the ground during winter: the bare, hard-pruned branches are quite architectural in themselves. When the pear trees have lost their leaves and the hydrangeas have been pruned to an attractive shape, there is a decidedly seasonal feel to the garden. The box, the paving and the fountain come into their own then.

HYDRANGEAS EN MASSE
are superb: the large, light green young leaves are as interesting as the flowers are beautiful – and particularly effective in a small, shady blind alley such as this (opposite page).

TO SOFTEN THE WALLS *of the penthouse, while enhancing the Mediterranean atmosphere created by the planting, two Greek oil jars were added (opposite page). Their lines repeat the curve of the stone balls that are the main decoration of the rooftop terrace.*

The fact that the soil in the raised beds could only be 500 millimetres deep is disguised by the careful selection of vigorous, wind-tolerant plants (following pages). Rosemary and Trachelospermum asiaticum are allowed to spill over the edges to complete the sense of a thriving garden – only partly an illusion.

IT'S ALWAYS A SAD moment when people move from their family home and large garden to a smaller place. The owner of this penthouse was reluctant to give up all connection with a garden so beds were included in the building's construction – to the engineer's specifications since the loading was considerable. I thought the design of the raised beds would work well for the kind of garden the owner envisaged: a flourishing, Mediterranean-influenced one with herbs and fruit that could be used in the kitchen. But anything planted up here would have to be resilient, for the wind is bracing, and kept restricted in height so as not to impede the view of the city. That translated into sections of strongly clipped bay trees (*Laurus nobilis*); lemon trees very horizontally espaliered against the low, protective wall that backs the beds; and rosemary (*Rosmarinus officinalis*) and *Trachelospermum asiaticum* thrusting forward at the front: all tough plants treated toughly, but sufficient to fill the two parts of the rooftop terrace with scent and colour and different textures – and to allow the owner to pop out to pick herbs and lemons, and trim and tend her garden.

The planting was satisfying to the eye but the L-shaped terrace needed focus. Any ornamentation would need to be earthy, in character with the planting; low, in keeping with the beds; visible from inside the penthouse because the terrace is too windy for much outside entertaining; and simple and contemporary like the penthouse architecture itself. Large sandstone balls of varying sizes, brought from India, proved just right. Strategically placed at the corners of bays constructed in the garden beds, two groups of stones to each part of the terrace, they added a little symmetry and a counterweight to the beds. I echoed their shapes in balls of English box planted above them. Landscape architecture and garden, ornamentation and planting – everything is balanced.

The stone balls rest casually on the paving, yet they assert an enormous pull: it's to do with their elemental shape and their relationship to each other. And their shape adds a softness too – something that people always want in a garden. As for choosing balls that would be in proportion to each other, and their setting – in the end it's an instinctive thing rather than a matter of mathematics: a feeling for harmony.

In the end it's an instinctive thing rather than a matter of mathematics: a feeling for harmony.

Acknowledgements

I would like to thank the following people very much for allowing us to photograph their gardens: Peter Alexander; Chrisy and Steve Angelo; Marilyn and Peter Bartels; Fiona Campbell; Cardinal Health; Fiona and Greg Carn; Nellie Castan; Megan and Paul Castran; Marina and Ken Davies; Kristine and David Deague; Ann and Michael Duffett; Andrea and Ron Evans; Jennie and Ren Falla; Helen and Tony Gandel; Andy and Mike Gibson; Matt Hanbury; Wendy and Richard Healey; Louise and John Higgins; Sue and Vic Kavals; Tracey and Chris Lucas; Ann and David Mattingly; Julian McCarthy; Joanna and John McNiven; Denise and John Nabb; Gaye and Gerry Paulusz; Maria and George Phillips; Lizzie Polk; Pat and John Poynton; Rosemary Richmond; Jaqueline and Denis Roche; Rosalie and Tony Roosenberg; Helen and Peter Sgro; Val and Jack Smorgon; Jenny and David Swann; Helen and Jim Thomas; Giselle and Ron Trower; Maria Valmorbida; The Wallace Apartments; Barrie Webb; and Michael Yates.

I would also like to acknowledge the help of Robyn Karas, who runs my office so diligently and coordinates the projects so skilfully; Alistair Bethke, Stuart Robinson, Martin Hopkins, Paul Shaw, Julian McCarthy and Andrew McFarland, who worked so hard on the creation of the gardens; and Amander Flaherty at Light on Landscape, who provided such excellent lighting designs for many of the gardens.

As well, I want to express gratitude to the whole Penguin team, with whom we work so closely and happily: Julie Gibbs, Executive Publisher, for her encouragement, love and ability to excel with every new book; Lesley Dunt, as ever the best and only editor a garden designer could want, for her help with the writing of the text; designer Tony Palmer for his ability to translate the essence of my designs to the page; Ann Ventham and Cora Roberts for their considerable help with the keying of the manuscript; Jane Drury for her meticulous proofreading; and Carmen De La Rue, Senior Production Controller, for ensuring the quality of the printed book.

I want especially to thank Simon Griffiths for his continuing and tireless efforts to ensure the photographs in our books are exceptional, and his great talent for seeing my garden designs as I see them.

Finally I would like to thank my friends Leonard Vary and Matt Collins for their continuing support and advice, and Peter Tsimilas for all his understanding during the preparation of this book.

Paul Bangay
www.paulbangay.com

Index

Page numbers in italic refer to photograph captions